The Shiloh Shepherd Story
Against the Wind—A Breed Is Born

Tina M. Barber
with Cinnamon Kennedy

Mid-Atlantic Highlands

Shiloh Shepherd Story: Against the Wind—A Breed Is Born

Copyright © 2006 Tina M. Barber

All rights reserved. Printed in Canada. No part of this book may be used or reproduced in any manner whatsoever without written permission except in the case of reviews or editorial reportage or commentary.

For information about all permissions please write to:

New Zion Shilohs
11922 North Road
Filmore, New York 14735

ISBN 0-9771978-1-6 Special Limited Edition
ISBN 0-9771978-2-4 Perfect Bound

Library of Congress Control Nos.
2006920209 (limited edition)
2006920210 (trade edition)

Editorial Coordination: John Patrick Grace and Willie Lass
Cover Design: Kathy and Larry Harris
Interior Design: Jennifer Adkins
Production: Kris Clifford

Mid-Atlantic Highlands
An imprint of Publishers Place, Inc.
945 4th Avenue, Suite 200A
Huntington, West Virginia 25701

Cinnamon Kennedy is a freelance writer in Black Mountain, North Carolina.

The text of this book is set in California Serif.

Dedicated to
YESHUA HAMASHIA
my Jewish Messiah and Savior.
*"For I am not ashamed of the gospel of Christ,
it is the power of GOD unto Salvation
to everyone that believeth."* Romans 1:16

Also, to my beloved grandchildren,
Joshua Daniel, David James, and Matthew Elijah
for their love of, and dedication to
the future welfare of
the real Shiloh Shepherd

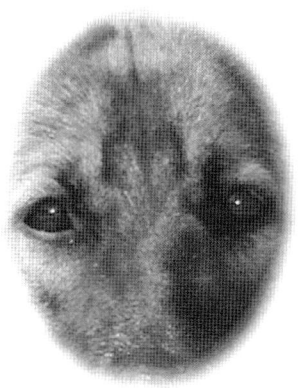

"Whoever says a dog has no soul has never looked into the eyes of a Shiloh Shepherd."

Foreword & Letters of Support

Although I had purebred dogs as early as 1937, my first German Shepherd Dog did not come along until a decade later, a magnificent, huge dog of unquestionable soundness of character and calm nerves. He was so big, he could look over the tallest easy chairs with ease, and would stretch nearly to the top of the door to signal that he wanted to go outside. We made jokes about formerly having lived a block away, but one night we tied him to the house and the next morning found our domicile on the next block!

He was the dog that caused me to fall in love with the breed. However, it was not possible to have the land and other things necessary for breeding until twenty more years had elapsed. That was when I moved to Toledo, Ohio, and began showing my own dogs in obedience and breed competition. I was good enough that others hired me to handle (in both types of rings!) for them. During the summers of the 1960s and early '70s I went to shows in nearby Canada nearly every weekend, and throughout the year in the Great Lakes region of both countries. It was during that time that I met Tina Barber, a young woman with a great love for dogs.

Over the years that followed, we kept in touch only occasionally. I had been saved in 1966, and when I learned that Tina had the same life transformation and assurance of eternity, we drew closer together. Our number of contacts multiplied. When I moved south and started judging for AKC, she asked me to judge and lecture at some of her Homecoming events. Eventually she got so turned off by the rejection of her ideas and the direction the American-lines GSD was heading, she decided to try making her strain of GSD into a separate breed. I watched the development of this Shiloh Shepherd breed-to-be over a greater period of time and with much closer contact than I believe anyone else in the sport has.

Tina has had the tenacity of a Bulldog, the energy of a Border Collie, and the determination of a German Shepherd in the pursuit of her goals despite several roadblocks and setbacks. She has a monumental job in attempting to bind disparate and novice forces into a unified society whose goals are matched to hers. Whether she lives long enough to see it realized, the fun and challenge may be more in the trying than in the reflecting upon any success. I pray God gives her long life to enjoy this pastime (which it can only be in His eyes) but more so to have an impact for Him, on the lives she touches through this endeavor.

—Fred Lanting
Author, *The Total German Shepherd Dog*

"I had the recent privilege of meeting Tina Barber; however, I have known many of her dogs through the years. They are some of the most majestic animals I've ever seen."
—Richard Sterban, bass singer for The Oak Ridge Boys

This book is probably unlike any dog book you have ever read. Words come to mind that one wouldn't ordinarily apply to a book about the development of a dog breed—rip-roaring, gripping, exciting—a spiritual and cynological thriller! But then, Tina Barber is no ordinary dog breeder. She has met and overcome a succession of disappointments, disasters, and betrayals, any one of which would have been enough to cause an ordinary dog breeder to give up.

The woman they call "Ma Shiloh" had a vision, a dream of a very specific kind of dog: big, beautiful, protective, intelligent, stable and manageable in temperament, an affectionate, trustworthy and loyal family dog. "A dog straight from the heart of God," in her words. She tried to develop a dog like that on her own, and failed. Then in 1974 her life changed and she tried it all over again with a different set of motivations. The results—the Shiloh Shepherds of today—speak for themselves.

Tina, born in Germany in 1947, has lived her entire life with dogs. Her grandmother trained guard and protection dogs. Tina's family came to America when she was eleven. She started her career as a Schutzhund trainer in her early teens, earned money as a show handler on the Southern Circuit, and did whatever she had to do to be with dogs, work with dogs, train dogs. Unimpressed with the lack of training and discipline of American dogs and their owners, Tina remembered her grandmother's protection dogs, especially one family dog named Rex, a massive, powerful German Shepherd. All her life she remembered that huge guard dog who could be safely handled by a small child.

Eventually Tina was led to the dogs that she needed to accomplish her goals and to fulfill her vision of a big, powerful, intelligent, great-hearted family guardian breed, a breed of dogs like Rex. But before that could happen she had to come to terms with the Lord. Even then, her trials had only just begun. For Tina was troubled, tried, beset and tested like Job.

The Shiloh Shepherd Story narrates with candor and frankness the story of how the Shiloh Shepherd dog came to be a living reality. Tina's story is fascinating. Few of us have any real conception of what is involved in the birth of a new dog breed, or the difficulties and setbacks that seem necessarily to go along with the process. Tina Barber's tenacity in pursuit of her vision, her refusal to give up in the face of adversity, make up the elements of an inspiring real-life drama of triumph through faith—in her God, in herself, in her dream, in her dogs. Tina's story has been an inspiration to me personally. I suspect it will be so to many others.

—Jeffrey Bragg, author, *Purebred Dog Breeds into the 21st Century*
and co-founder, Seppala Siberian Sleddog Project
http://www.seppalasleddogs.com

This book gives the reader a good look behind the scenes, at what it takes to actually develop a new breed. This book is not just about a dog, but all of the dogs that contributed their genes to make a mark on the real Shiloh Shepherd for decades to come!

This book tells the complete story, starting with the memories Tina brought back from Germany and her experiences with the many variations of the GSD in America, which led to her desire to produce better hips and larger dogs for her training program. The book shares her disappointments with some of the litters she was producing and about many of the dogs she was raising and training. It walks the reader right into her testimony and the pact she made with the Lord in 1974. From that point on it covers the trials and triumphs that she had to deal with along that road, sort of like the Biblical exodus through the wilderness. The reader will be witness to the battles that she had to deal with in the Promised Land, since the formation of the ISSR and SSDCA. The book paints the truth about her friendships and the betrayals she had to endure.

This book not only shares short stories about some of the dogs that set the foundation for this breed, but it also covers things that have never been revealed before. It's an emotional roller coaster that takes you on an unusual, rare journey; it is a book that people will have a hard time putting down until they finish the story! And yet it's not fully finished. All the Shiloh breeders are still living it, and many people will want to watch them as the journey continues toward this breed's full recognition. Like a marathon race, those that are not running it will still want to see what happens at the finish line.

You will cheer on the breeders of Shiloh Shepherds as you read this book, and will develop a kindred spirit for the REAL Shiloh Shepherd. You will laugh with Tina and her breeders, cry with them, and when you are finished reading the truth—STAND with them!

—Laura Kathryn, Lic. ISSR Breeder
Solace Shilohs
http://www.solaceshilohs.com

Table of Contents

Foreword & Letters of Support..v

Acknowledgements.. xi

Introduction..xiii

Chapter 1: Seeds of a Breed..1

Chapter 2: Finding My God, Finding My Calling..19

Chapter 3: Building a Firm Foundation..38

Chapter 4: Challenge and Change..60

Chapter 5: New Directions..82

Chapter 6: Breeding Amid Dissent..104

Chapter 7: Out of the Ashes..122

Chapter 8: Old Friends, New Beginnings..141

Chapter 9: Final Steps..164

Appendix: Shiloh Shepherd Breed Standard..177

Acknowledgements

After devoting nearly a year of my time into a possible documentary project that failed, I felt totally drained and a bit irritated at the thought of having to pour my soul out again for something even more complex.

That is why I want to thank Willie and Yvette Lass for not giving up on me, but pushing me forth despite my reservations.

Once we announced this project on our Shiloh Shepherds Community Forums, the support was electrifying! Many of our members offered to help in any way they could, and I want them all to know how encouraging their enthusiasm was!

Kathy Harris, who is presently raising her second ISSR Shiloh Shepherd, even got her graphic-artist husband Larry to help out with the cover design, and he did a wonderful job!

Special thanks must also go to:

Karen Ursel, who tirelessly typed and retyped proofed manuscript sections. She also helped me research the sidebars and find and select the proper pictures for each chapter. Most of this work was done at our local Flying J's, where the staff kept the coffee coming!

Corinne Filipski's help was invaluable as she continued to proof and reproof many portions of this manuscript in order to spot obvious technical errors. Her insights regarding the data being presented also helped me to prevent any possible reader boredom!

Laura Kathryn dedicated many hours into cross-checking, looking for any minor changes so that I could reproof the entire manuscript one last time before it went to the printer's.

I would also like to thank Jenn Diemert and Lilli Anglin for taking the time to proof the final manuscript and provide me with some excellent feedback.

Their combined efforts were invaluable in helping me to meet all of the publisher's deadlines. Without their specific contributions, this book most certainly would not have been completed!

Most of all, I would like to take a moment to thank all of the unnamed prayer warriors from coast to coast who stood in the gap for this book and all of those that were involved with this project! I am certain that their prayers helped all of us to stay focused despite the horrible anti-Tina campaigns being instigated by the dark side in order to stop the truth from being published!

Heartfelt thanks to my collaborating writer, Cinnamon Kennedy, for picking up the pieces of my story, sifting them, and then weaving them into something that I hope you'll agree makes an interesting book and is easy to follow.

Last but certainly not least, I want to thank all of the ISSR breeders that have continued to uphold their commitment and loyalty to a higher standard in order to produce the best quality puppies they can! Their children and grandchildren will be able to proudly point back at the pioneer spirit their ancestors possessed because they had the courage to stand strong for what they believed in! You should be proud because your support is enabling this breed to survive for future generations to enjoy.

Editor's note: The author and publisher agreed that a number of pictures of less-than-ideal quality had to be included in the book because of their historical value or because they helped to tell part of the story. Many of Tina M. Barber's best pictures of the Shiloh breed's development were lost in the fire that destroyed her house.

Introduction

The year was 1974. I was in a converted barn in Palmyra, New York, working with a dog named Tammy, who I thought might make a good Schutzhund dog. She had passed to the point where she was working with a real decoy, and he was trying to agitate her—and succeeding. I thought Tammy had some potential. But at that moment my hopes were not too high.

It was one of the lowest moments of my life. I was married to a violent drug abuser. I had two young boys whom I was raising virtually alone. I supported our family with my job selling Kirby vacuum cleaners, and I used every precious spare moment to work with my dogs. I had been working with German Shepherd dogs since I was a child in Germany, but by that point, my efforts seemed to have come as far as they were going to go. I was selling "personal protection" dogs for thousands of dollars apiece, but I was also running into canine hip problems so severe that I was sometimes forced to give my valuable dogs away. And I was beginning to think that the German Shepherd breed was problematic itself—in addition to health problems, many of the dogs had serious problems with temperament.

I had been breeding my own dogs for a while, in hopes of solving these issues, and after several years of intensive research, I had come up with some innovative ideas about ways to overcome hip dysplasia. But none of my fellow breeders wanted to listen to a "geneticist" with only a ninth grade education, and the problems with the German Shepherd were too big for me to tackle alone. I was seriously considering giving up on dogs.

Tammy was eleven months old when I took her up to the Schutzhund training facility to try her out, to see how she would do as a protection dog. I had brought my little son Johnny with me, who was then just two years old, and I had set him up playing with trains behind the barn while I worked with Tammy.

When you are raising a puppy for Schutzhund training, you have to be prepared to do formative testing. If the pup has good prey drive, and shows an aptitude for the sack, he or she can participate in some agitation sessions with a real decoy. If the young dog can handle these sessions without showing any fear, then formative training can commence. At that point the decoy will agitate your dog practically into a frenzy, in order to encourage a good full mouth bite on the sleeve. Nipping is not acceptable; that's why the sessions have to be intense. That is also why the decoys wear lots of heavily-padded protective gear.

Tammy was coming out really well at the decoy. She had absolutely no fear. All the other trainers that day were impressed by her ferocity. Teeth out, very courageous, clearly confident that she could tear the decoy to shreds. I watched as the decoy went for a pass at Tammy. She ran out like a bolt of lightning to jump him, growling, her teeth flying. Then, without warning, my two-year-old son came out of nowhere. He ran up and grabbed the dog.

It all happened so fast there was nothing I could have done to stop it. There was no way a dog in that state of frenzy could be expected to do anything but bite Johnny to death. I had seen dogs worked up to such a pitch that they would even turn and bite their handlers if they got too close.

But this dog, Tammy, just stopped. She stopped in mid-air to avoid hurting my baby. Instinctively Tammy knew the difference between an enemy and a child, and she knew how to switch gears in a fraction of a second. I hadn't seen that kind of a reaction from a dog since I was in Germany. It was an incredible moment. I thought, Here is a dog like the ones I remember from my childhood! And I have this dog's gene pool—and I can develop it!

At that moment I understood that this dog represented my life's pursuit.

At that time I had no idea that the dogs from the Tammy line would become the celebrated Shiloh Shepherds, dogs so intelligent, so sought-after that they would triple German Shepherd prices and be in demand that was constantly higher than supply. I didn't know that I would soon be running ads in *Dog World* magazine guaranteeing Shiloh Shepherd dogs with "Sound Temperaments in Super Size, with Awesome Hips"—and running those ads for thirty years. I didn't know that I would be called upon to lecture on genetics from some of the most prominent breeders in America.

At that moment, all I knew was, I don't care what the public thinks, this is the way I'm going to go.

All dog breeds were developed by people. The variety and specificity of type in purebred dogs would not have arisen without humans picking and choosing dog pairings, evaluating characteristics that arise from each and every breeding, and then pairing the next generation of dogs carefully

Tina and Tammy, 1974.

in order to bring out certain traits and to eliminate others. In many cases, breeds of dogs were developed by individuals who devoted their lives to the project. The German Shepherd was founded by Captain Max von Stephanitz in Germany in the early 1900s. The Jack Russell terrier was founded by Reverend John Russell in the mid 1800s. The Doberman was founded by Louis Doberman in the 1800s. Every modern dog breed has a story to tell. Through diligence, perseverance, divine blessings and luck, I can say that I too am the founder of a new breed of dogs. There are not many people alive today who can say that. And so far as my publisher and I know, this is the first memoir of a breed founder ever published in America.

The history of the Shiloh Shepherd is intertwined with my own story, a story that goes back even further than the years of my life. My family has been raising and training old-style German Shepherds for nearly 100 years. The Shiloh Shepherds of today actually started with my attempt to re-create my grandmother's extra-large German Shepherd dogs, which were famous across Germany and Poland. This is the story of my development of the Shiloh Shepherd, an intelligent, strong, magnificent breed of dog, and of the many trials and heartbreaks that came along the way.

Two-year-old Festus (Gunsmoke's son) with four-year-old John, 1976.

The Shiloh Shepherd Story

Chapter 1

Seeds of a Breed

Germany—The Early Days

My grandmother, Wanda Schoenhals, was a dog breeder in Poland and Germany from 1919 to 1956, a time when a woman dog breeder was an extraordinary thing. My grandfather died when my mother was still in her early teens, and my grandmother took over all his businesses, including a coal delivery business, several apartment buildings, and the breeding of extra large horses and extra large dogs. She was a heavyset person, very tough and independent. People were in awe of her: here was this older lady handling huge Belgian horses and vicious German Shepherds as if it were a normal, everyday thing! My grandmother Wanda was a very powerful woman. I have been told that I take after her.

My grandmother's businesses were in Poland, in a border town called Lotz. She and my mother went back and forth frequently between Poland and Germany. One day they met a German man who was a master trainer, specializing in police and protection dogs. He told them that he was looking for quality dogs that he could train for his program. He had searched all over Germany for good breeders, and everybody he met had referred him to a certain German woman in Poland who was breeding Belgian horses and giant German Shepherds! My grandmother invited him to see her dogs. He thought they were amazing. Right away he started a program for her to supply him with a steady stream of dogs. At the same time he met my mother, and the rest is history. That man was my father, Wilhelm. From 1935 to 1964 he was heavily involved in training German Shepherd dogs.

Wanda and Anita with their horses, 1938.

World War II interrupted a period of happiness and prosperity for my family. My grandmother and father had been doing very well with their linked businesses, and my mother acted as secretary. But with the war, everything changed. My grandmother started to lose money because so many of the people that she had done business with were in the concentration camps. Eventually the authorities took over my grandmother's apartment houses. I still recall my great-grandmother telling me stories of how my grandmother gathered up all of her jewelry, diamonds and gold, and sewed them into the hem of her coat.

Then the day dawned when the authorities came for my grandmother, and she put on her secretly-jeweled coat and went with them. They put her on a train headed for Belsen, but by some miracle on the way her train was intercepted, and she got out. She was taken instead into Germany, where she was put in Watensstedt-Salzgitter, a lower-security displaced-person camp, from which she and her daughter managed to escape. She had lost everything, though my grandmother, always the businesswoman, got into the black market almost immediately, selling coffee and chocolate. My father caught up with her, and even shared in some of her business ventures. In this way they managed to make back some of the money that she had lost, but things were never the same. World War II was a sad time for my family, as it was for many other families in Europe. My mother loves to watch the movie *Schindler's List*, because she lived through some of that.

I was born in 1947, in Gebhardshagen, near Heidenau, a small town outside of Toschtedt, near Hamburg. As far back as I can remember, animals—lots of animals—were a regular part of my daily life. We lived in suburbia, but a kind that's a lot different from suburban America. Dogs were always in the

Although the original *polizeihunde* did not gain popularity among the civilian breeders prior to World War II, through the efforts of Mr. Ing. Karel Hartl (since 1955) in the development of the Ceskoslovensky vlcak, an intense, controlled program for the ultimate border patrol dogs was started, producing dogs that were virtually indestructible.

Since its earliest days, civilian breeders have been fascinated with the Ceskoslovensky vlcak but were unable to obtain breed recognition for many years. The problem was the Cynologic Organization in Czechoslovakia. They had refused to recognize a breeders' club and enrollment of the pedigree. In 1982 they gave up, but thanks to the efforts primarily of Mr. Ing. Karel Hartl, the breed was officially recognized with the first forty-three dogs being enrolled. During the next ten years (1982 to 1991) 1552 puppies were enrolled. Since then, this amazing breed has gained popularity in Europe as a wonderful family companion and protector, like the early GSD's used to be, and as an especially excellent search dog, surpassing even the GSD in this regard and all existing working dogs! We would like to thank Mr. Pavel Hanuska for permission to share these two pictures of the Ceskoslovensky vlcak at work.

Ira z Litavske Kotliny

Kelt z Molu Es

house, and cats were always outside. I remember sneaking out to the pasture and jumping on the big horses bareback and riding them with no halters. I remember hand-feeding the baby goats. We also kept chickens, and lots of pigeons. We didn't live on a farm; that's just how everybody lived, even in town.

Tina with her goats in Germany, 1952.

My favorite animals were always the dogs. All the dogs were bred and trained to be useful. They were city dogs with all kinds of functions, including recreational ones. I remember that in Germany men would get up early and put on their heavy boots and raincoats just for the fun of tramping around in the field, laying tracks for the trained dogs to follow.

In Europe at that time, if you had a business that required delivery, you kept a dog with you to protect the money. My grandmother trained her dogs for protection, and her delivery drivers took her dogs in their coal trucks on all of their delivery runs. The older dogs came to protect the drivers (and the money), and the puppies rode along to be socialized and trained. When those puppies had received their own training, my grandmother sold them as protection dogs to most of the other businesses in town. I remember seeing one of her dogs protecting the town bakery. Just about every business in town had one of my grandmother's dogs, except the milkman—and that was because he used a Rottweiler to pull his cart.

My grandmother's dogs were much bigger-boned than the modern German Shepherd. They were calmer and more stable, but also more deadly. They were thinking dogs, with super, almost human intelligence. Any of those dogs would have given his life for my grandmother without question.

My memory of my grandmother's dogs is the reason that I focus so hard with the Shiloh to keep that sharp intelligence, because it's a unique thing. German Shepherds, back in those days, could be trained to climb trees and to climb walls. They were just amazing animals.

The one that I recall the most was Rex, our house dog. He was a bi-colored German Shepherd, a very big, massive dog, probably 135 to 140 pounds. He was bigger than the male Rottweiler that lived up the road who used to come over and play with him. Rex was very blocky, with a square head, mostly black, just a little bit of tan on his feet and chest. He wasn't as tall as a Shiloh today; I'd say about 28 inches. But he was a massive, powerful dog, a lot like Ch. Red Rocks Gino, pictured on the back cover of *The Complete German Shepherd Dog* by Bennett, Denlinger, Paramoure and Umlauff. Yet I could handle him easily, even though I was then a small child.

***

Unfortunately, our good times in Germany didn't last long. When I was nine, my grandmother left Europe for America by boat, and shortly thereafter my father left the country.

In 1958, when I was eleven, my mother and I left for America too. I was already upset about the changes that had taken place in my family, but the hardest part about moving abroad was that we had to leave Rex in Germany. He stayed with relatives in Europe, because he was too old to cross the Atlantic on a boat. I didn't want to come to America if it meant leaving Rex behind, so I left in an angry mood.

Our ship cast off from Bremerhaven on my voyage to America, a voyage which took ten days. We were on a huge military ship, with bunk beds everywhere. The boat was packed full of German and Polish immigrants. The only interesting thing I can recall was discovering Coca-Cola! It helped to settle my stomach, and it gave me an appreciation for this unique beverage that I have enjoyed ever since. But those ten days were the longest time that I have been apart from German Shepherd dogs to this day. I missed Rex, and I missed the way things used to be.

Somehow I knew that America would be completely different, and I was right—it was.

America—A New Frontier

Our boat docked in New York City, and we were picked up by my grandmother Wanda and my aunt Sophie, whose husband Stanley did the driving. I had been used to doing most of my traveling by wagon or train, so it was a unique experience to spend nearly seven hours in the back seat of a large American car. Our destination was Rochester, New York, where my grandmother lived.

In Rochester I was enrolled in a Catholic school. I was eleven, and I should have been in fourth grade. But I couldn't speak the language, so they put me in a second grade classroom with these little kids, at tiny little desks! I was a big person for my age, which didn't help matters. I was nearly five feet tall, so sitting in a little second-grade desk was terrible for my self-esteem. I was so angry and embarrassed. I think that's why I lost all of my German. I started becoming English-oriented, because I wanted to fit in better.

But at the same time, I had no respect for the people I was meeting, so I didn't really want to fit in with them at all. I didn't know where I belonged. I grew rebellious, and developed lots of animosity. I hit puberty at about the same time as I came here and got put in second grade, so you can imagine what a nightmare that was. I spent a lot of time in the movie theaters to escape, as well as to improve my English. It was easy to relate to movies like *Rebel Without a Cause* with James Dean.

I started getting into fights just because I couldn't speak English. Anybody who tried to give me a hard time about anything was not cool in my book. I wasn't impressed with America. For a brief, lonely time, there were no Shepherd dogs in my life. Only my grandmother's silly fox terrier!

And I was shocked when I first saw dogs in the parks in Rochester, pulling their owners around on a leash. I could not believe my eyes. I thought to myself, Incredible! A person puts a dog on a leash and the dog drags them down the street? That's ridiculous. In Germany our dogs were precision military trained. You didn't a need leash, because the dog was expected to heel without one.

Even then it was clear to me that I understood dogs better than most Americans did. Like my father and grandmother before me, I knew I had a talent for working with dogs. But I was just a lonely pre-teen kid. What good would that talent do me if I couldn't even use it?

Schutzhund—A "Natural" Is Born

One day in Rochester, I met some friends of my father's who had also come over to America from Germany. One of them, Nero, was running a Schutzhund training academy, the first one in America, in Palmyra, New

York. He invited me out to see his facility.

Schutzhund is partly personal protection dog training, partly precision obedience training, and it also involves tracking. It consists of three parts and three levels of excellence as goals. In Germany, Schutzhund is a sport that Germans use for all dogs—practically every tiny town in Germany has a Schutzhund club meeting twice or three times a week. I honestly think that Schutzhund is more popular in Germany than baseball is in America. It's a sport, but it's taken very seriously. It's also useful: Every German Shepherd dog in Germany has to prove that he is a working dog. They have to be titled in obedience, protection and tracking before they can get their breeding papers. That's what Max von Stephanitz wanted when he developed the German Shepherd breed.

So, of course, many Germans that came to America had started training their dogs for the sport, just like in Germany. Then some American people got involved too—Schutzhund is really very interesting—and things caught on. I was lucky to be in on it from the beginning.

The Schutzhund club in Palmyra was located at Nero's huge farm. It had a big dairy barn that Nero had converted into a training facility; boarding and breeding kennels were at the bottom, and the whole loft was an indoor training field. The big pasture outside was our outdoor training field.

Those old German men took me under their wing, because my dad wasn't around. At that time women were not accepted in Schutzhund, and I don't think I would have been accepted if I had come in as a twenty-year-old or a thirty-year-old. But I was a kid. And I was their friend Willie's kid. They all felt sorry for me, and they kind of adopted me. I was just barely in my teens when I started training and eventually titling dogs.

A wealthy man from Texas named George Theriot got interested in the sport and came to visit my father's friends in Palmyra. George drove a Cadillac convertible with big cow horns on the front. He was a real Texan! But he got excited about the sport of Schutzhund. He got a couple of dogs for himself, and he ended up being the founder of the North American Schutzhund Association in America, the first official organization for American Schutzhund. That association is still going today. George set up trials and competitions for the dogs, and he did all the funding. Of course, the men that were running little American Schutzhund clubs, most of whom had come over from Europe, were thrilled. The whole group of these men would come and work out their dogs at the farm in Palmyra. Then we would travel around the country, and go to Dallas, Texas, for the Schutzhund trials sponsored by George Theriot.

George Theriot was an exceptional man, and will continue to be sadly missed by all of those that have ever had the opportunity to get to know him. I recall many gatherings in his home in Dallas, where he would share training stories as well as his famous Texas jokes, always with the same serious tone that had you holding your breath, waiting for the punch line. My all-time favorite went something like this...

Did you ever hear about the Texan that went to visit Fort Knox? Well, as he waited to enter, the guard took a few moments to explain to him what he was about to behold. With excitement in his voice he said, "You know, sir, we have so many gold bars in here that if you wanted to you could easily build a wall, four feet high, around the entire state of Texas!" The Texan stood still for a moment, thinking it over, and then replied, "I'll tell you what, son, you just go ahead and build that wall, and if I like it, I'll buy it!"

Yet when it came to his dogs, he was extremely serious and had a relationship with them that was not surpassed by many. I recall the time he asked me to help feed his dogs. We walked into his huge garage-kitchen-grooming room-kennel and he took me to the counter, where he showed me what portions each dog should get. Then he told me to "ask" the boys to bring their dishes. Each one walked up to me holding his dish! It was my job to fill it and set it on the proper (named) placemat. This process was repeated until all five of his fully trained stud dogs received their dinner. I have never experienced anything like that prior to or since that day.

George Theriot, third from left, back row. Tina Barber third from right, back row.

Training a dog for Schutzhund involves a lot of precision: perfect heel, perfect sit, perfect recall, dumbbell work, all very intense; also bite work and tracking. All of this involves hundreds of hours of training. For example, in dumbbell work, you toss the dumbbell, the dog has to go over the jump, pick up the dumbbell, turn around, go back over the jump, and sit square in front of you. Getting the dog to pick up the dumbbell is one thing. Getting the dog to go over the jump to get to the dumbbell is not too hard either. But a trainer has to put hundreds of hours of extremely specific training into the simple act of getting a dog to go over a broad jump, pick up a dumbbell, and then come back over the broad jump. An intelligent animal would rather walk around the jump. The trainer must teach the dog to deny his own instincts and to obey commands instead.

Tracking is the part of Schutzhund in which dogs are trained to track with their noses on the ground looking for articles; it's very useful if you ever lose your keys in the woods. I would say it takes three or four hundred hours to get a dog to pass the FH (tracking) trials and get properly titled.

The main part of Schutzhund is the courage test. It sounds easy, but it isn't. It goes like this: You come out on the field, heeling with your dog. Your dog is off lead, of course, at a heel. You see a decoy coming out from behind a blind, the length of a football field from the other side, and he comes running towards you. You calmly say *fass*! And your dog takes off like a bat out of hell, runs across the field, until he reaches the decoy, then it's kind of a mass collision. The dog attacks the guy and rips him apart. (Well, since the guy is a decoy he's all padded up so the dog doesn't actually do any damage.) And then, it's one command—*aus*—and the dog has to release. When the guy gives up, the dog releases him and sits and watches him. If the guy moves, the dog re-attacks. It is mainly fully controlled bite work where the dog has to show his bravery.

Then the dog heels next to his handler while the decoy is in custody, and the dog is taken back to the judge. This is called the transport. At this point the dog can't show any aggression, unless the decoy attempts to escape.

Normally, dogs take almost two years of consistent work from puppy tug play until a dog is ready to complete all of his Schutzhund titles and earn good scores.

As soon as I discovered the world of Schutzhund training in America, I devoted myself to it. I spent most of my time in the Schutzhund field. My grandmother gave me her Corvair because she didn't know how to drive and didn't want to learn. By the time I was fourteen I was driving her car from the inner city of Rochester to Palmyra, New York, for Schutzhund trials. I had found where I belonged.

In Europe I was watching my father train dogs even before I was five years old. At sixteen I degreed my first dog in Schutzhund. In the end I degreed fourteen Schutzhund dogs for George Theriot's NASA. It wasn't even official when some of my dogs were titled; tallies weren't being kept until 1971, I believe, and I began titling unofficially in the fall of 1967. Between then and 1976 I titled fourteen dogs. I'm proud that I was able to degree these dogs at such a young age, but what I was looking for more than anything else was respect from the senior Schutzhund trainers, to show them that yes, I could do it, even though I was a girl.

> After an earlier, brief attempt in 1969 to introduce the sport of Schutzhund in the United States, the North American Schutzhund Association was founded in 1971 by Alfons Ertelt (who later started the American Temperament Test Society), Karl Marti, George Theriot and others. The name was soon changed to the North American Working Dog Association.
>
> Taking a more American slant on things than the Schutzhund groups that were to follow, their program was geared for the "Complete Working Dog." Emphasis was placed on stable, well-trained dogs with the trainer/owner working and communicating with his dog as a team rather than doing just attack or bite work. The program was described as a natural progression after earning AKC/CKC Obedience titles. NASA offered licensed trials for the U.S. and Canada with internationally recognized degrees for ScH. I, II and III and the INT (International Working Dog Degree). The trials included tests in tracking, advanced obedience/agility and controlled protection work. At one time NASA was the third largest dog organization in North America, with a newsletter, *The NASA News*, published annually, but by the late '80s it had been supplanted by more European-oriented Schutzhund organizations.

NASA logo

Teenage Years—The Other Side of the Fence

My happiest memory from the '60s is probably of Lady, an extremely intelligent light black and tan bitch, who was my best friend from 1962 until her death. No matter where I went, before I started to drive, especially if it was to the kennel or the stables, I had to take Lady with me. If I left her at home and my mom needed me for something, she would just send Lady out to find me. That dog could track me down no matter where I was. It didn't take me long to figure out that if I wanted to stay "lost" I had better take my dog with me—especially if my friends and I were planning on riding our bikes down to the beach to check out the boys!

I stayed in school as far as ninth grade, but my heart was never in it. I was living with my grandmother. I got into a bunch of fights, and into problems at school and outside of school, and even earned myself a juvenile police record. High school was just not where I wanted to be.

I got involved with the German Shepherd Dog Club of America in 1965. I just hung around at the club meetings, at the bowling hall outside of Rochester. When they needed demos done I would go there and help out. They all knew I was good with the dogs.

At the same time I started bringing in money of my own. I wasn't a highly educated person, but I am a workaholic. I sold Avon when I was fourteen, to pay for some of my dog expenses, and I haven't stopped working since. I used to skip school and go down to the stables and take out trail rides for money. And when I wasn't at the stable I was at the kennels, training dogs for a growing list of clients.

The president of the German Shepherd Dog Club of Rochester at that time hooked me up with the owner of a local kennel who was trying to expand. Immediately I offered to help clean her kennels and groom her dogs for free, just so I could be near these beautiful animals. It didn't take long before she practically adopted me. I had some dogs that my German friends had given me, but I couldn't keep them at home because I lived in the city with my grandmother and four dogs, so she let me keep them at the kennel where I worked. I would go there before school and after school to see them, and to do kennel work.

In 1965 Val, a solid, black long-haired import ("Konigin's Black Velvet"), joined my pack, then another dog, King, who was a bicolor grandson of Red Rock's Gino. He could not be shown, but he was an excellent demo dog on my team. The last one to join us was Kim in 1967.

These three dogs plus Lady became my spectacular foursome. The five of us traveled all over the country doing "Team-4" demonstrations that everyone loved to watch. Here's how they went: I would enter the arena with Lady and Val on my left and King and Kim on my right, all in perfect heel formation. After about forty paces King and Kim would go into an automatic down, while I moved forward another forty paces. Then Lady and Val would go into an automatic sit. I would continue walking, then turn and give the first group a signal to recall, while the second group continued to sit. King and Kim would trot over to me and then sit in front of me. Then I would give Lady and Val a hand signal to down, then to crawl forward, then sit, then start toward me, then drop again. I would leave King and Kim in their positions, then walk toward the other two and stop in heel position. It was nothing more then some fancy obedience commands, but they were done in tandem with four dogs, so everyone thought it was amazing. We also performed a Schutzhund routine for larger events. Those four dogs were great friends to me; we all understood each other very well.

"Teaching" Instead of "Training"

Eventually people that were in the German Shepherd Dog Club of Rochester started hiring me to train and show their dogs for them. Even though I was young, I was working with some of their dogs, and they saw that I was winning shows because my dogs behaved better. So a lot of the other breeders would say, "Well, gee, what's your secret for getting your dog to do this, that or the other?" That opened up doorways.

Training is not so much teaching the exercises; it's building a relationship with the dog in which the dog respects you. If the dog has no respect for a person at all, it's because the person doesn't project an aura of "I'm the boss, you're the dog, that's the way it is, let's move on." A dog needs that security. It's like a child needs to know, "I'm the police officer, and you'd better listen." If your attitude is, "I'm trying to be your friend! And I'd like you to listen to me!" the dog goes, "Yeah, right, in your dreams, sucker."

The handlers who were training the Schutzhund dogs, who came over here in the '70s, the macho men, did a lot of very hard, heavy-handed correction. The Koehler method got to be very popular, because it got results. But it was basically beating the dog into submission: "Do it or I'll kill you," instead of, "Do it because you respect me, or you know what's going to happen if you don't." It's a completely different attitude.

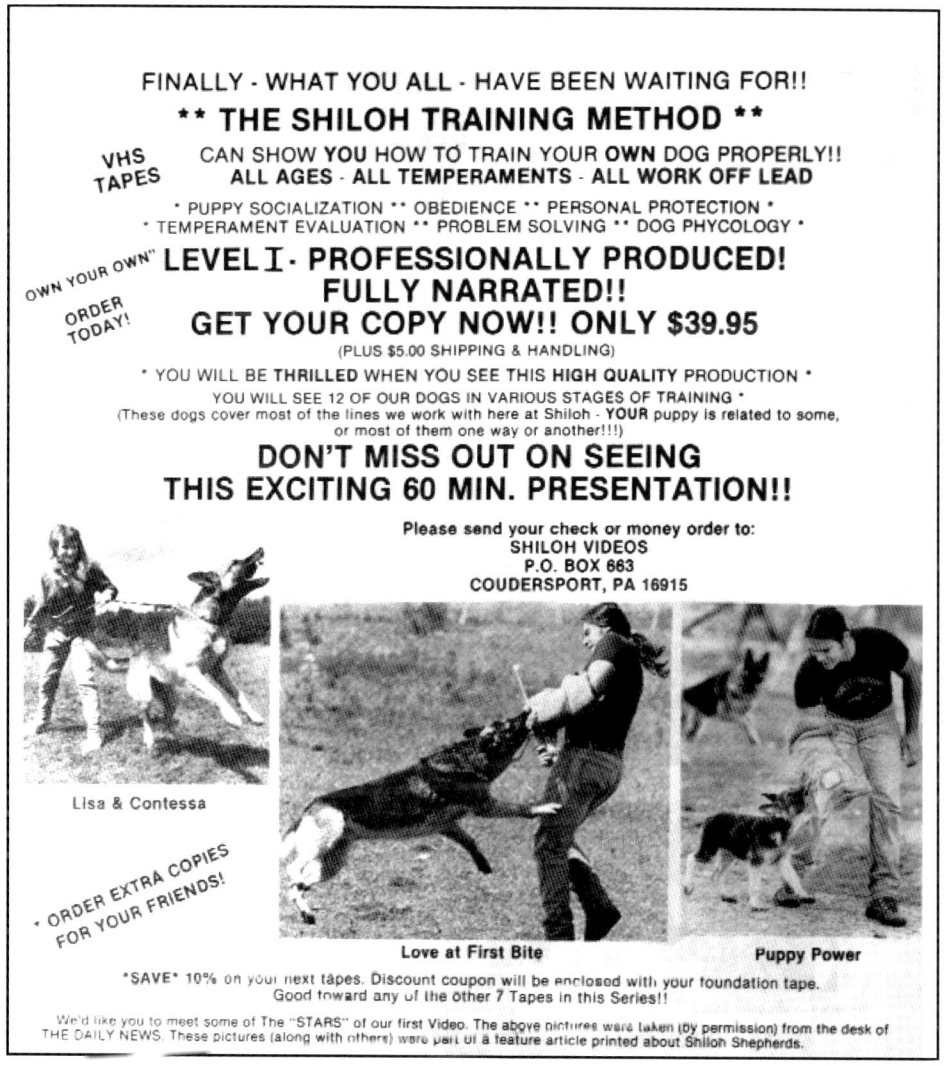

Shiloh Training Method Video Ad

In a wolf pack, the "alpha" does not mean the boss, the dominator, the abuser. It means the provider, the leader, the one everybody looks up to, the confidant, the security. This is what a wolf pack expects from the alpha: The alpha's going to lead us, he's going to protect us, he's going to feed us, he's going to take care of us. Yes, he can tell us to back off, he will control us like a parent does a child, he will have some rules that we must follow, and he will discipline us if we break them. But it's a benevolent relationship, and it's consistent.

It's not like humans, who abuse that position, and apply the wrong pressure, and actually make their animal disrespect them, because the dog starts wondering if the human is nuts. A dog might end up thinking, "What is your problem? If I'm allowed on the bed, then I'm allowed on the bed! If I'm not, I'm not! Make up your mind! Because I'm beginning to think that I don't trust you. And if I don't trust you, I'm not going to listen to you, and if I'm not going to listen to you, why should I want to follow you?"

My philosophy about dog training is not complicated, and it's not abusive. If dogs are handled correctly, it's amazing what they can do.

The Southern Circuit

I got pretty involved in showing dogs in my teenage years, and that made me drift a bit from my true love of Schutzhund. Money is a big motivator. People who are into showing dogs have enough to really spend on their dogs, and to spend on their handlers, and I was a natural dog handler.

I passed my ninth grade tests, but I skipped most of that year at school. In tenth grade I stayed in school for two months, so I could quit at sixteen. I had already titled my first Schutzhund dog, so school didn't impress me much. As an adult I got my GED, but that was by the skin of my teeth, too. I know a lot of things, but I learned them all through experience!

Back then, I was working on being the best dog handler in the business. I had a nice body, I impressed the judges, I knew how to run in the ring. My bust size and mannerisms seemed to get the old judges' attention, and I won a lot of shows. My dogs behaved well, and the way I dressed in the ring kept the judges' eyes on us. I was known for spending the day outside of the ring in cut-off hillbilly jeans, and then I would wrap a tie-off skirt around me to go into the ring... it did get a lot of attention! But I think the biggest reason my dogs did so well is because they were so well trained.

In the winter I would do a lot of Southern circuit dog shows. I left mid-January for the Southern circuit, and practi-

Tina on the road in 1963.

cally every weekend there was a show: Greenville to St. Augustine, then from Pensacola over to Lafayette, and then we went up through Memphis, and then over again to Knoxville. The shows would often run Friday, Saturday, and Sunday. Then on Monday I would recoup, Tuesday I would hit the road, Wednesday or Thursday I would arrive at the next show grounds and get my dogs prepared, and then Friday, Saturday and Sunday we would do the show. After the show I would just load up the station wagon and drive on to the next place. I was only fifteen, and I did this circuit with four to six dogs per trip.

I didn't have my driver's license yet, so I borrowed the driver's license of a nineteen-year-old, blonde, blue-eyed girl named Shelly. That's how I got around. At fifteen I looked like I was eighteen. I've always looked older than my age, which was a handicap in fourth grade, but an advantage at age fifteen.

I got twenty to thirty dollars per show for my handling fee, because I would show four dogs a day. That was a lot in the '60s, and that's the kind of money I was making. All my expenses were paid to go to the shows, so I would sleep on the beaches with the dogs, and then I'd take a shower in the rest area truck stops by the sides of the highway. And then I'd pocket the hotel money too! So I had a regular business going back then.

I remember one time I walked into a Pontiac dealership in Rochester. I spotted a Buick Riviera, and said, "I want that car." The guy didn't even want to talk to me, because I was barefooted, and wearing my trademark cut-off jeans and a funky hillbilly top. (This was my "Daisy Mae from the Dukes of Hazzard" look.) I asked him how much the car was, and I think he said it was fifty-six hundred dollars. I said "What do I have to do to get it?" He said, "You have to come up with the cash!" I told him okay, and I started pulling out hundred dollar bills from my pocket—I had like six thousand dollars throughout the pockets of my cutoff jeans. That's how much money I was making.

That was the beginning of a winning streak in my life. As a gifted teenager working in a field that's dominated by adults, I was writing my own rules, and succeeding. I didn't really have what you might call "teen years," except for a few bouts of police problems, but I made up for that by getting rich, and doing what I enjoyed.

But just when I thought I had it made, tragedy struck.

My grandmother died suddenly on May 10, 1965. I was seventeen. I was at the playground with my dogs, babysitting my cousin George, when I got a call that my grandmother was in the hospital. On her deathbed she told me that she was going to be with the Lord. She said that her fight here was over, and her battle had been accomplished, and she was ready to go home. I couldn't accept that. I prayed to God to let her live, and she died.

I could not believe that a loving God would have let that happen. I had flashbacks of the nuns I had dealt with at Catholic school, the ones that threw my baloney sandwiches out on Friday, because they would rather see a child skip a meal than eat meat on a Friday. If that's who God was—a tyrant who liked to watch kids suffer, while taking the life of such a good woman—then I did not want anything to do with Him.

On My Own

At that point I became more rebellious than I ever had been before in my life. My grandmother was the only thing besides the dogs that held a semblance of sanity for me. When she died, I was basically on my own at seventeen. I started living at the kennel, and then I just kind of bummed around from kennel to kennel, and got involved with all the dog people. I did a lot of floating. After my grandmother died, I had no use for religion. I thought it was just a bunch of bogus baloney. I was in control of my own life, and would make my own rules! I got into fights and started running with a wild crowd. I broke horses during the day and worked as a go-go dancer at night.

But for all my wild living, most of my time, energy, and money were still spent on the dogs.

I got heavily into the dog show world at that time, because there was so much money to be made there. I liked the money, but compared to my Schutzhund experience, the show dogs were dumb. They were "Foo-Foo" dogs who could run pretty, and yes, I could train them to behave well, but most of them didn't have a brain between their ears. The Schutzhund dogs were the heart of what a dog should be, but the "Foo-Foo" dogs were where the money was. So it was a tug of war for me. It's not hard to figure out that the Shiloh Shepherd is a combination of the good qualities of both the show dog and the Schutzhund dog. The Shiloh is a pretty dog, but it's got to have the brain, and the ability to be a good family protector as well as a good friend. I like to describe the Shiloh Shepherd as "the total dog, bred for beauty, brains, and brawn."

Through my show experience I met hundreds of important people in the dog world. I worked with many famous handlers, trainers, and breeders whom I met at the shows, and I learned a lot from them. I met Fred Lanting in the mid-'60s, and he became one of my mentors and a good friend. I met Jimmy Moses, the number one German Shepherd handler for decades, when he was technically still a kid.

Then, after four years at my first kennel, I began to see that something was wrong. The woman who ran that kennel was spending a fortune on her dogs, and I was showing them for her, but something was off: the dogs weren't winning.

Being the competitive person that I still am, I was saying, Wait a minute, hold the phone here. I'm not going to go in there and take second, third or fourth. I'm not that kind of person! If I'm going to put the time and energy into training a dog, I want to win. I've got to go with somebody that's going to pick the dogs that can win, or I'll pick them myself. I asked the woman who ran that kennel if I could pick some dogs for her, but she didn't trust my judgment because I was so young, so she and I eventually parted ways.

The woman who ran that kennel spent a lot of money breeding and showing her dogs, but she got dogs with a lot of health issues, because she was buying them for their names. I learned a lot from her, but unfortunately it was her wasted money that taught me the lessons. Even as a teenager I knew that famous names don't guarantee good progeny, and sometimes it's quite the opposite.

Around this time a woman named Carol Petranto let me pick a German Shepherd for her to show on the AKC circuit. That dog, Gunsmoke, went all the way to the top. After that, people started hiring me to pick dogs, because I could spot the winners.

My personal life remained hectic. I got married in 1967, which was a mistake. That marriage was annulled just over a year later. In 1969 I married Rick Barber. I had been running a kennel in the city, in a house that I was renting just outside of Rochester. His sister was my roommate, and he started hanging around and I couldn't get rid of him. That's really how it all started. We got married in September 1969. My son Richie was born on July 7, 1970, and my second son, John, was born on June 10, 1972. My grandmother had left me quite a large settlement when she passed away—almost half a million in today's dollars, which was held in trust for me until I turned twenty-five. I purchased a new ranch home in a very nice, small estate settlement and continued to work with my dogs.

I knew that working with dogs was what I wanted to do with my life. By my early twenties I knew how to buy dogs, how to train dogs, how to show dogs, and I was taking my first steps as a breeder. At the time I figured that I would use my talent for working with dogs to support myself, and maybe to improve the German Shepherd dog world.

I had no idea how big my project would become.

Gunsmoke.

Chapter 2

Finding My God, Finding My Calling

Konigin Kennels

When I began breeding German Shepherd dogs, I made a decision that I was going to develop my own type of dog: a German Shepherd like Rex, the dog I remembered from my childhood in Germany. I had been using the name "Konigin," which is German for "Queen," as my kennel name since 1962; it was my dream that Konigin dogs would be "real" German Shepherds—big, intelligent, and strong, but not overly aggressive.

I had researched all of the top kennels around. I'd seen a lot of dogs at the shows, and I'd been picking puppies for other people, so I knew what I wanted. I already had a Liebestraum female (for intelligence) and a Wikingerblut female (for Schutzhund), and now I wanted to expand. I added Osnabruckerland (for size) and Piastendamm (for courage and "heart"). I liked what I was seeing in the whelping box.

I had good reasons for wanting to develop my own dog. If you really study German Shepherds year to year, they don't look anything today like they did thirty or forty years ago. The type has completely changed. There is the German German Shepherd; there is the Czechoslovakian version of the German Shepherd; there's the UK version, which used to be called the Alsatian, which has the stocky, low-stationed bodies; there is the White Shepherd; and there is the long-haired German Shepherd. And they're all called German Shepherds. They all carry the same name, but they're all different.

Although the European version of the German Shepherd Dog has managed to maintain a reasonable degree of consistency, in America and Canada there are many "types" of German Shepherd Dogs, all registered with the AKC/CKC under one breed name even though they vary greatly in size, temperament, coat type and structure, as well as other qualities.

Here are just four examples taken from the standard "smooth coat" variety. Long coats are also gaining popularity, and although they may somewhat resemble the plush-coated Shiloh Shepherd, they are much smaller in size.

Low-stationed   Tall, leggy   Farm Type   Over-angulated

Ideal Shiloh Shepherds

Laz (plush)   Luke (smooth)

As for the American German Shepherds, I saw them splitting into two distinctive types. The dogs imported from Germany were aggressive and increasingly difficult to handle. On the other side were the German Shepherd show dogs—smaller, finer-boned animals, which in my opinion were lacking in intelligence and nerve. A German Shepherd is not supposed to be overly aggressive, but it shouldn't be a timid dog, either. Who needs a dog that rips up the back screen door so can he can crawl under the bed if a gun goes off? That was not what I was looking for. I wanted a dog that was very responsive, and very intelligent, that had the guts to deal with a situation if it really came to it, but that didn't look for trouble. And I didn't think that the modern

American German Shepherd was that dog.

My feelings about the future of the breed began to cause controversy in the German Shepherd world. I took to writing articles about the faults I was finding in the breed. My German Shepherd breeder friends were not exactly happy with my analysis.

But it was too late to go back. My mind had started clicking: I need to breed my own shepherd. What I was seeing out there was not what I wanted. It was almost like a fashion model who can't find dresses in the stores that will make her look good.

Josh and London

Then one day she says, "I'm going to start designing my own." I figured that if I had my own stock, I could also improve the hips so they wouldn't break down on me, and I could maintain the temperament I wanted.

By now I knew that breeding wasn't easy, but I wasn't intimidated. Though I was young, I had already worked with some of Germany's greatest trainers, as well as with some of America's best breeders. I was sure that once I figured out my "secret formula," there would be no stopping me.

Then, to my frustration, hip dysplasia knocked my confidence away.

I would spend nearly a year raising and training one of my puppies for someone, devoting at least two to three hours per day to active training and socialization. Then, without warning, the dog would start limping. At that point I would slow down the training procedures, hoping the problem would correct itself, but often it did not. I lost a lot of my training time, and a lot of money, to bad hips.

Canine hip dysplasia really motivated me to fight. When those excellent dogs would all of a sudden become too crippled to continue the grueling work that Schutzhund demands, I finally saw that I had a mission.

In spite of the combined efforts of the Orthopedic Foundation of Animals (OFA) and the German Shepherd Dog Club of America, who were urging all breeders to get hip x-rays of their stock before breeding, the problem was expanding out of control. Breeders were checking their dogs for dysplasia, but even dogs with good hips were producing dysplastic puppies. For a while more than half of the German Shepherd pups born had some form of hip dysplasia, and less than 4% of all GSD's born were getting OFA (passing) hip certification. It seemed like the more everyone checked the hips, the worse the dysplasia was getting! Breeders were obsessed with breeding champions to other champions, and without warning, recessive genes for hip dysplasia had flooded the gene pool.

Something was very wrong.

Holy Hill

I had realized what I wanted to do with my life: breed the perfect dog. But at the same time I came to that understanding, I realized that the rest of my life was falling apart. I was going to improve the German Shepherd breed—a nearly impossible task—and that didn't scare me. But I also had to improve my life. That seemed harder.

I had always worked part time in sales, to raise extra money to fund my work with dogs. Whenever I had free time I would sell stuff: Avon, Singer sewing machines, Fine Arts china, Lifetime cookware. When my son was a baby I began selling Kirby vacuum cleaners in people's homes, and by the time our family moved out to a Rochester suburb called Hilton, I had my own Kirby vacuum center in town. At that time Kirby salespeople were averaging a sale for one out of every six calls; I had been averaging 4.5 out of six consistently. I guess I am a natural salesperson. I used to bring the dogs into the Kirby center and work them in town while I was manning the store. I'm not one to waste time.

When Rick and I bought our house in Hilton, New York, the realtor warned us that the area was nicknamed "Holy Hill" because there were religious fanatics living all over the place. I laughed and told the realtor not to worry—we were pretty tough! My husband was a black leather jacket biker, and I raised protection dogs. I didn't think we were in for much trouble from a bunch of Christians!

Rick was working at Kodak, making good money, but everything he made he blew on drugs. We weren't hurting for money, because of what my grandma had left me, but he was going through it like water. I mean, he was buying cars, and he was buying motorcycles, while I was supporting the family. He was spending more than he was making, and it was getting very stressful. After he got fired, things got a lot worse.

Rick was into bar fighting and brawling. He was a very dirty player—you know, "drugs, booze, and Harleys"—one of those kinds of guys. He had "Born to Raise Hell" tattooed right down his arm. He was a wiry man, not a huge, muscular person, but he was quick, agile, and he had some basic karate type of moves. People were afraid of him. If you wanted to beat him, you had to really be dirty about it, because he could be dirtier than you were. He was the kind of guy who would grab a pool stick and clean out the bar. I once saw Rick whip four men at one time.

I spent more and more time with the dogs, just to get away.

Challenging Canine Hip Dysplasia

When I first started breeding, all I knew was, I've got to get rid of this dad-gum hip dysplasia, I can't take this. I didn't know how I was going to do it, but I was going to do it.

I was fortunate to be able to work with a lot of professional breeders who had been breeding puppies long before I came along: Betty Mott of Emmview, Priscilla Mooney of Ensomhed, and Fred Lanting of Von Salix. I worked with a lot of experienced breeders who had excellent reputations. Betty did quite a bit for me, especially while I had small children. She helped me establish my gene pool base, and I am very grateful to all the people who helped me. I think that is why I have always tried so hard to help other people who want to get started in breeding.

But I soon found that hip dysplasia was an extremely tricky problem. Canine hip dysplasia is a little like diabetes. If you're genetically prone to being a diabetic, you don't want to raise your children eating candy and drinking Coke all the time, because they're more likely to develop the disease than a child who is raised on fruits and vegetables. The genetic factor is the key, but there are environmental factors involved too, and that's why hip dysplasia is such a complex thing to analyze.

I'd breed two dogs whose parents' hips were good, whose grandparents' hips were good, and whose great-grandparents' hips were good, of course thinking I'd get good hips in the puppies. But I wouldn't. This would happen constantly, and it didn't matter what gene pool I worked with. In some of these litters, seven out of ten puppies would come up dysplastic no matter what I did. Breeding several generations of OFA good or excellent dogs seemed to lower the percentages, but even so, hip dysplasia refused to release its grip.

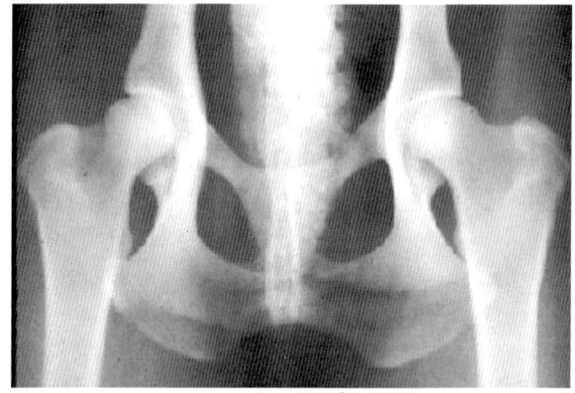

OFA good.

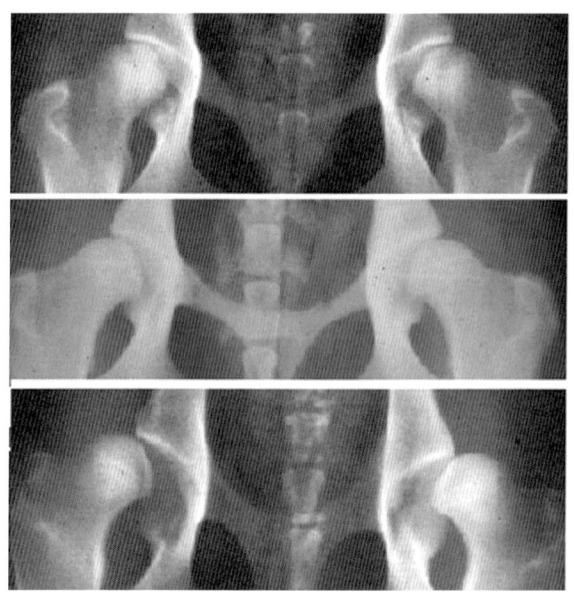

Examples of CHD Grade 1-2-3.

Not being a patient person, I decided to investigate my litters as well as those of my co-breeder friends. Between all of us we had accumulated a great deal of information. Since most of our dogs were show dogs, breeding dogs, or in my Schutzhund training program, the only ones we did not have x-ray information on were the puppies that were sold as pets. In those cases, we called the owners to have their puppies x-rayed. Sometimes we actually went to their homes, picked up the dogs, and brought them to the clinic. Dr. Nundy, my vet and mentor, offered his assistance at cost. It was an exciting project, and we all started to feel like the saviors of our beloved breed: we were going to find the answer!

My breeder friends and I examined hundreds of dogs before we saw a pattern emerging. We looked for common ancestors in the first seven generations, hip ratings in the first four generations. Then we looked for common denominators between those with good hips: size, coat, nutrition, stress, carefully looking for a possible environmental key to this puzzle, as well as a genetic one. Fred Lanting, the expert on German Shepherd dog hip dysplasia,

> Long recognized as an accomplished all-breed judge, and one of the foremost authorities on German Shepherds and canine HD, Fred Lanting is also a leading canine consultant and lecturer, has experience as an assistant in veterinary surgery, and has judged prestigious shows in thirty countries for FCI, AKC, UKC, and other registries.
>
> He has been involved with dogs since childhood, is a long-time GSD breeder, has participated in the show world as a handler and judge since the mid-'60s, and has trained and titled many dogs in Schutzhund. He is one of only two judges in the U.S. approved by the SV. He is the author of numerous books and articles, including *Canine Hip Dysplasia* (2005) and *The Total German Shepherd Dog*. Both are available from the author at mrgsd@hiwaay.net.

Fred Lanting, Don Robinder and Fran Attridge evaluate GV CH Zion's A-Tribute to Snow's Grizz, Homecoming 2001.

became my mentor when it came to hips. I would often send him x-rays and say, "Okay, tell me what you see in here." During the next four decades, Fred Lanting, my Christian brother and CHD mentor, became an invaluable source of support.

At the same time, I had noticed an unrelated problem that other breeders were having with the smooth versus plush coat in their dogs. Plush coats are unacceptable for German Shepherd show dogs, and the plush gene is recessive. But breeders would breed two smooth coat dogs and end up with plush coat puppies. If you bred two plush coats, you would never get smooth coat puppies: the plush coat was a very powerful recessive! So I saw the frustration of show people who were moaning, "Jeez I had seven puppies, and four of them are plush-coated, even though the parents weren't!"

That's when I started looking even more closely at littermates. It was becoming clear that most of my lines had a strong plush coat genotype. Whenever I bred smooth coat dogs that had plush coat littermates, I found many plush coat pups in my litters. When I bred dogs that did not have any plush coat littermates, I usually got full litters of smooth coats. When I bred dogs that did not have any plush coat littermates for three to four generations in their pedigree, the pups were almost always smooth coated! Could the trait have been eliminated? If a breeder could easily eliminate the plush coat gene by breeding only dogs that had no long-haired littermates, then if we bred dogs with no dysplastic littermates, maybe we could eliminate hip dysplasia! I needed to find some strong lines that were producing a lower incidence than the rest, and go from there.

I was excited about the possibility, and I wanted to start working on it right away. But it turned out that since compiling that amount of data would require the assistance of other breeders, it would be no easy task. In order for the plan to work, all breeders would have to be very open about the amount and frequency of hip dysplasia in their pedigrees. But breeders were cagey about how much dysplasia they had in their kennels. With such a high percentage of dysplastic dogs, and with dog prices closely linked to hip ratings, the breeders had an incentive to hold their cards close to the chest. The sincere cooperation from the breeders was the only thing that could allow us to continue to document hundreds of litters, and to find out once and for all which lines had the lowest incidence of dysplasia. Without the breeders' cooperation, our new program was doomed to fail.

Unexpected Changes

Sometimes in the evenings, as I sat at my kitchen table scrutinizing pedigree upon pedigree, there would come a knock at the door. As our realtor had predicted, the crazy Christians in our neighborhood tormented us for months, knocking on our door to witness for Christ. They were always met by Rick, who was usually in a demonic-drug crazed mood, and by several attack dogs.

They kept coming back anyway.

I thought they were a bunch of self-righteous phonies, and I was starting to feel trapped in my home. The realtor had warned us what would happen, but I guess I didn't realize what I was getting myself into.

My babysitter, who lived across the street, was a Christian, and all my other neighbors were constantly coming over to witness. At first I allowed them into the kitchen to sit down, and they would go through their shpiel, and I would tell them "I don't want to hear it." We'd have some dialogue going back and forth, in which I would try to counteract their testimony, but it never seemed to set them back. I would tell them, "You can't prove the Bible is true!" I stuck to my guns, and they stuck to theirs. After a period of time I wasn't even allowing them to come over any more. Nothing irritated me more than the sound of one of them knocking on my door.

But at the same time, I was also getting a weird sense that something was starting to change in my thinking.

Even though I was still so young, I supposed I had gotten hardened over my lifetime. Many of the things that I believed in as a child, and that I was told by various people, I found out later were lies. I had turned into a hardened, calloused person. "Do unto others before they do it to you": that's a comfortable slogan that hardcore people like I was tend to latch onto.

Certain things that those Christians said, things that I was carefully not listening to, would come back to my mind, and they would bother me to the point where I would want to find out the truth about them. They talked a lot about the Bible and God's love and about prophecies, and some of these things I wanted to research, but I didn't understand anything in the Bible. Of course, I didn't want to ask those people either, because I certainly didn't trust them. I wanted to find out for myself.

Things got even stranger. I'd wake up at night remembering certain verses that those people had said. I felt I had to prove to myself that this was just some kind of big scam, that I wasn't stupid enough to believe what some person told me. I was a leader, after all, not a weak, gullible fool!

This war inside of me grew stronger and stronger, as my husband got worse and worse. Things were coming apart at the seams, in my marriage and in my life. The Christians kept coming over to witness, and I screamed for them to leave me alone!

I guess I was starting to feel God's hand in my life. It felt scary. My marriage was falling apart, my dog breeding was having a rough go, and I was thinking a lot about myself: I was a good person, wasn't I? Granted, maybe a bit wild, but I was honest. I didn't steal or cheat. I worked hard, I took pride in my accomplishments. What was going on with me?

LMX

To take my mind off everything that was going on at home, I started the LMX (LitterMate X-ray) program, a complicated system for organizing and referencing littermate x-ray and other pertinent information in my dogs. The LMX program is still in use with the Shiloh Shepherds today.

When I started the program, everybody thought it was a big joke, since I was far from a certified genetics authority. But I figured, if I couldn't get all the data I needed to finish my research into hip dysplasia from other breeders, I was just going to have to breed more puppies and get the data myself. When I sold someone a puppy, I would tell the new owners, "You have to x-ray the puppy's hips at one year and give me the x-rays for my records." I would make them sign contracts with me: you've got the puppy, you owe me the x-rays when the dog is a year old, or you owe me $500. In some cases I would actually hold back papers until they brought me the puppy's x-rays. These days, things like that are not so unusual, but back then some people thought I was a nut.

I got other data for my program by backtracking: I knew who some of the ancestors of the dogs in my kennel were, and I called around to get the hip data of as many dogs as possible in their ancestry. Right now in the Shiloh shepherds LMX program I have all the data from 1967 forward, and I have some data from as early as 1962, from some of the dogs in the background of our gene pool. Forty years of x-rays is the reason why I can now feel confident about the hips in the Shiloh Shepherd breed.

The LMX program evaluates lots of different criteria—temperament, height, weight, color, coat, sex, structure, health issues, and hip reports, not to mention documenting the dominant and recessive characteristics of all the littermates. I did not put much emphasis on "show" faults in my LMX records, which set me apart from most other breeders right away. I wanted big, intelligent, reliable animals with good hips; things like length of tails were not really my main concern.

***

As the LMX program took shape, I kept breeding more and more dogs, trying with each litter to get closer to my goals. But as my goals became clearer, achieving them seemed farther away. Breeding dogs is a genuinely difficult thing to do.

I learned from my mentors that you will see the "shadow dog" in your gene pool a lot more often then any of the dogs listed in your pedigree. The "shadow dog" represents all the recessive traits that you will not see in your dog, but that you might see in your dog's offspring. I started doing comparisons of littermates in order to track down the stronger lines: if a litter of ten puppies had only one with bad hips, while another litter of ten puppies had seven bad hips, it was an indicator of the parents' strengths and weaknesses.

Various recessives are carried by each pup, but the problem is, you can't see them. You won't know which dog picked up which recessives until they are bred, and if the recessives from both sides happen to "click," you may be in trouble. The only way to hedge your bets is by studying the lines carefully and profiling the possibilities.

One time I looked into my whelping box after a certain litter was born. I thought, "Well, this is strange!" Two of the puppies in the box, a brother and a sister, were solid blacks. I knew that their parents were dual-colored, and their grandparents were dual-colored, so the last thing I expected to see was a black dog, let alone two! I researched the dogs' pedigree, and I found solid black way back in the gene pool, once in the fifth generation and twice in the sixth generation. That's it. It was way in the background of the gene pool, and it showed up in my whelping box. How did it get from there to here?

I started tracing to try to find the answer. I contacted people that had dogs that came from these breedings, and as usual, my LMX data came in handy. Tracing the pedigrees back, I found that Afra (Ursa's grand-dam) was solid black, and she did have three black littermates, but she showed up only once in the dam's side. The two blacks in the sixth generation on the sire's side shouldn't really have influenced this litter, but they did!

The Shiloh Shepherd Story

Sample pedigree

Grandparents	Great Grandparents	4th Generation	5th Generation

"Quality German Shepherd Dogs Bred to Work and Win" Exclusively since 1962

SIRE

Shiloh-Di-Mar's Cujo
AP-28",140 lbs.
..t.B/T,Med-S
X-G 8 mo.
LMX-O-D(1L-7)
..t.pig.Mono.
Huge sz.brd.hd.
Very hvy bone
Med-S,med-H
Temps,Gd.ang.
Easy trained
Very high int.
Sup.movement

SHILOH SHEPHERD'S

LINEBRED:
Zeus 5,5,5-4,4
Lance 6,6,6-5,5
Paladen 5-5
Dexel 5-5
Gunsmoke 4-4
Rude 4-3
Max 3-3

DAM

Shiloh's Our Image of Ursa
27",85 lbs. B/Cr.
Med-S, X-G 2 1/2 yrs.
LMX-O-D(1L-10)
Huge sz.Gd.pig.
Gd.hds,No LC
Super hips
Ex.OB pros.
Super temps
SchH pros.
Pos.herding & S & R

Shiloh's Apache Joe
27 1/2", 126 lbs. B/Cr.
S.Q. Med-H,X-G 3 yrs.
LMX-O-D(4L-32)
OFA GS-13102 Hvy bone
LC res. Monorchids
Med-Lg sz,Brd hds.
Sup. temp & hips
Exc. SchH pot.

Dimar's Sheba von Shiloh
27",115 lbs. B/T P.T.
Med,X-G 2 yrs.
LMX-1-SP(3L-19)
Lt.pig.LC res.
Huge hds. Hvy bone,
Med-S temps
B/S,Sup OB prosp.

Shiloh-Ensomhed The Gator
27",118 lbs. B/T
Med-S,X-E 1 yr.LC res.
LMX-O-D(1L-7)Gunshy/Ln
Lt.pig.Huge bone,
Brd.hd.Aloofness,
Produces excellent hips

J-N-J's Nikki von Shiloh GT
26 1/2",80 lbs. B/S
Med-H, X-G 2 yrs.
LMX-O-D(4L-32)
Full sister to
Apache Jo & Ch.Ptd.
Chance,Sup consistency
Gd.pigmt. Gd-sz-hips-temps

Shiloh's Max von Glendhenmere
26",92 lbs. B/RT P.T.
Med. X-G 4 1/2 yrs.
LMX-O-D(1L-5)Sm sz/lnbd
Monorchids & LC res.
Drk.pig. Med-S Temps.
Super hips & temps.

Shiloh's Ursa von Ensomhed
28",126 lbs. Lt.B/S
Med-H, X-E 5 yrs.
LMX-O-D(3L-26)
Lt.pig. Poor ang.
Huge sz. Sup.hips &
temps.(Full sister to Luke) Soft ears

Portrait of Fabrena
26 1/2", 95 lbs. B/T
Med-S,X-G 3 yrs.
Lt.pig.,LC res.
Hvy bone, Brd.hds.
Gd.conf.Gd.hips,
Med-S temps.
Kaleef's Rude-Da-Paulo
27", 105 lbs. B/RT
Med.X-G 3 yrs.
Perfect conf.Brd.hd.
Gunshy,monorchids
P.T.AKC # WD651045
Von der Lins Ursa Major
27 1/2", 114 lbs. B/T
Med-H,X-G 3 1/2 yrs.
Huge,B/S,Brd.hds.
Monorchids,LC res.
Sup.int,sup.temp.

Shiloh's Max von Glendhenmere
26",92 lbs.B/RT,P.T.
LMX-O-D(1L-5)Sm/sz.
Monorchids & LC res.
Drk.pig.Med-S temp.
Super hips &temps

Shiloh's Ursa von Ensomhed
28",126 lbs. Lt.B/S
S.O. Med-H,soft ears.
LMX-O-D(3L-26)
X-E 5 yrs.

US/Can Ch.Shaft of Delshire
26 1/2",100 lbs.
Drk. B/RT, Med.

Danlyn's Ka Ja CD Sch1
AD AP-25",70 lbs.
Drk.B/T ,Med-H
OFA GS-7459-T

Ch.Campaigner's Gunsmoke
27", 115 lbs. Lt.B/Cr
Lt.pig. Str.front

Von der lins Ursa Major
27 1/2", 114 lbs.B/T
Med-H, X-G,B/S,Huge

Kaleef's Rude-Da-Paulo
27",105 lbs. B/RT
Med-S X-G 3 yrs.Perf.conf.
Brd. hd.
Von der Lins Ursa Major
see above

Ch.Chardo's Fu-Ku
AP-28" 110 lbs. B/T
Med,X-G 2 yrs.Sup.int.
Typy to Lance
Ch.Be Ha Le's Lil Whisper
AP-27",90 lbs. B/T
X-G 2yrs.Lt.pig.
Gd.conf. Exc.mover
Zeus of Fran-Jo ROM
AP-26",85 lbs.B/RT
#1 sire for '77 &'78

Faulen Fortune of Victrix
AP-27",90 lbs.B/Cr,Lt.pig
Prod.huge bone,gunshy
Zeus of Fran-Jo ROM
AP-26" 85 lbs.B/RT

Von der Lins Fan-C GT
AP-27",90 lbs. B/T
X-G 5 yrs.
Can.GV US/Can Ch. Shaft of Delshire
26 1/2", 100 lbs.Drk.
B/RT,Med.hvy boned

Danlyn's Ka Ja CD SchH 1
AD AP-25",70 lbs.
Drk.B/T, Med-H,OFA

Ch.Campaigner's Gunsmoke
(see above)

Von der Lins Ursa Major
27 1/2",114 lbs.B/T
Med-H,B/S,X-G,Brd.hds.

Ch.Zeto of Fran-Jo ROM
AP-26",95 lbs. B/RT
Pam of Fran-Jo
AP-25",80 lbs. B/T
Lex von Haus Dexel CD
AP-27", 95 lbs. B/T OFA GS-3297
Tolopat's Legend of Danlyn CDX
AP-25",70 lbs. B/T OFA GS-2158
Ch.Eko-Lans Paladen ROM
AP-27", 110 lbs. B/Cr.
Campaigner's Flying Nun
AP-26", 80 lbs. Lt.B/Cr.
Zeus of Fran-Jo ROM
AP-26", 85 lbs. B/RT Brotner to Zeto
Von der Lins Fan-C GT
AP-27",90 lbs. B/T X-G 5 yrs.
Zeus of Fran-Jo ROM
AP-26",85 lbs. B/RT
Faulen Fortune of Victrix
AP-27",90 lbs. B/Cr.Lt.pig.
Zeus of Fran-Jo B/rt
Von der Lins Fan-C GT

Ch.Gordic aus Nordan SchH III
AP-28",105 lbs. B/T OFA
Chardo's Cadence
AP-27", 95 lbs. B/T
Ch.Amber's Gilli of Will-We's
AP-27", 100 lbs. B/T
Ch.Barkley Square's Whisper
AP-26", 85 lbs. B/T
GV US/Can Ch.Lance of Fran-Jo ROM(325
B/T Fortune-Elsa
Ch.Mirheim's Abbey ROM (96)
B/T (Lance-Amber)
Fro pf Fran-Jo
Linebred Troll
Lee Ray's Convictrix

GV US/Can Ch.Lance of Fran-Jo ROM
Ch.Mirheim's Abbey ROM
US/Can Ch.Vero of Bihari Wonder UDT
Cara-Mia's Afra (blk) hard.

Ch.Zeto of Fran-Jo ROM
AP-26",95 lbs. B/RT
Pam of Fran-Jo
AP-25", 80 lbs. B/T
Lex von Haus Dexel CD
AP-27", 95 lbs. B/T OFA GS-3297
Tolopat's Legend of Danlyn CDX
AP-25",70 lbs. B/T OFA GS-2158
Ch.Eko-Lans Paladen ROM
AP-27",110 lbs. B/Cr. Morgan-Lanc
Campaigner's Flying Nun
AP-26",80 lbs.Lt.B/Cr.
Zeus of Fran-Jo ROM
Von der Lins Fan-C GT
AP-27",90 lbs. B/T X-G 5 yrs.

Shiloh Dimars Cujo

CODE CHART

LINE 1: *HEIGHT, WEIGHT, COLOR

*AP = approximate (Listed where no actual records were taken.)

Color Codes:
B/RT = Black and Reddish Tan	LT-B/S = Light Black and Silver	BRN/SBL = Brown Sable
B/GT = Black and Golden Tan	DRK-B/S = Dark Black and Silver	CKL/SBL = Chocolate Sable
B/CR = Black and Cream	LT/SBL = Light Sable	GLD/SBL = Golden Sable
B/S = Black and Silver	GRY/SBL = Grey Sable	DRK/SBL = Dark Sable

LINE 2: TRAINING, TEMPERAMENT, HIPS/AGE*

*Age last x-rays were taken.

Codes: Training	Temperament	Hips	
P.T. = Protection Trained	Soft	X	= X-rayed
G.D. = Guard Dog	MED-S = medium soft	E	= Excellent
S.Q. = Schutzhund Quality	MED-H = medium hard	G	= Good
H.D. = Herding Dog	HARD	SP	= Still permissible
S.R. = Search & Rescue	Please see temperament analysis on	D	= Dysplastic
	collage for complete description.	S.D.	= Severely Dysplastic

LINE 3: LITTERMATE X-RAY (LMX) INFORMATION

LMX (This litter was x-rayed) -0 (0 or 1 etc.,) -D (dysplastics in litter)
(Parenthesis)number of litters-number of dogs x-rayed

EXAMPLE: LMX-2-D(3L-28) = This breeding had 2 dysplastics out of 3L (3 litters) -28 (28 dogs x-rayed)

PLEASE NOTE: Any litter where less than 80% of the progeny have been x-rayed would not be considered an LMX litter. Occasionally a dog will be accidentally killed or the owners have moved out of contact so information is difficult to obtain. If the litter consisted of 8 pups and we have information and x-ray plates on at least 7, we consider that an LMX litter.

LINE 4: FAULTS PRODUCED

LINE 5 etc.: DOMINANT AND RECESSIVE GENETIC QUALITIES PRODUCED

LINEBREEDING CODE:

EXAMPLE #1: Lance 3,4,4 - 5,7,7,8,8,9
The above example would mean Lance was on the SIRE's side once in the 3rd generation and twice in the fourth - on the DAM's side once in the 5th, twice in the 7th, twice in the 8th and once in the 9th generation.

EXAMPLE #2: Paladen 3,3 - 4,5
Paladen is on the SIRE's side twice in the 3rd generation - on the DAM's side once in the 4th and once in the 5th generation.

EXAMPLE #3: Luke 2 - 3
Luke is once on the SIRE's side in the 2nd generation and once on the DAM's side in the 3rd generation.

That's an example of how I continued to be surprised with almost every litter. Just as in the human world, where no two individuals are exactly the same, so it is with all of nature. There is no way you can predict everything. It is commonly thought that pups will resemble their parents, but the fact is that most puppies do not. Every litter born will display some new trait that was passed down from one of their ancestors. When I began to apply statistics from my LMX research to my breeding program, slowly things began to make more sense.

In order to understand the shadow dog, I worked furiously on my kitchen table in the evenings, compiling, analyzing, and categorizing pedigrees. Six, seven, eight generations—I compared, contrasted, and researched why my puppies were ending up with the conditions that they had. I spent a lot of time calculating probabilities, looking for the shadow dogs before they showed up in my whelping box. To my frustration, I was still seeing stuff I hadn't expected, and much that I certainly hadn't wished for.

Mister

Mister came from an elite line of German import dogs: I paid four thousand dollars for him as a puppy in the fall of 1969. Then I spent the next two years training him and caring for him.

One of the most important things my father taught me was to overtrain a dog for Schutzhund: make sure the dog is ready for his "3" before you enter him to title for his "1." In other words, make sure he's ready for the hard test before you even give him an easy one. I only titled Mister through Schutzhund 1, but he was fully trained through Schutzhund 3. Since I had so many people wanting to breed to him, I figured I would get his OFA done, so I could start collecting some stud fees even before I finished putting him through all of his degrees.

The OFA certificate, from the Orthopedic Foundation of Animals, is to certify that a dog's hips are okay before he is bred. I went to the vet and had Mister's hips x-rayed without thinking much about it. But the vet called me in his office and said, "You want to look at this, Tina?"

I couldn't believe my eyes. Mister's x-rays clearly revealed that his hips were completely out of their sockets. Severe remodeling had already started to set in because his acetabula were too shallow to support the femoral heads. With grade-3 dysplasia, most dogs would have had a hard time walking, much less performing in a sport that always puts such a rigorous beating on a dog's body. Mister would go straight up a six-foot scaling wall for me. You've got to have hips to put you up there! He was a good dog, and wanted to please, and he must have had an extremely high tolerance for pain.

After nearly three years of raising and training, Mister failed his hip x-rays in the spring of '72, and I retired him to a life of leisure on a farm. All of that hard work, and thousands of dollars, all gone in the time it takes to x-ray a dog. Training a dog to Mister's level takes a lot of dedication. It's like building a car from scratch, and then totaling it on your first drive. Mister wasn't the first dog that I lost to hip dysplasia, and he wasn't the last. But he was one that just about broke my heart.

Lowest Moment

It was not long after the disaster with Mister that I realized that for all my work, Konigin Kennels was a flop. I was obsessed with producing the perfect dog for my needs: super intelligence, huge size and great hips, plus a "look" that would stop traffic. But no matter how hard I tried, I just couldn't do it.

I would get huge size, but the hips would fall apart. I would get super intelligence, with good hips, but they would be small, ugly, foxy-looking dogs. I would get looks, with no brains! A few nice ones would raise my hopes, but then they would produce absolute nightmares.

In the beginning I was very excited about being a breeder, and I told everyone "I'm going to do this, this, and this"—then I found out it's not that easy. Things didn't happen the way I thought they were going to happen, and it was costing me a fortune. I really wasn't sure what to do. I was making good money with my sales career, but I was getting frustrated with my dog breeding.

I was about to say, The heck with it. It took less than a decade to wipe out half of my inheritance, and I still couldn't see my goals coming close to fruition.

My kennel was a mess. The dogs had bad elbows. They had bad hips. They had many different health issues. I tried all the different German lines, I was trying some of the most popular import lines, I was trying the American show dogs, and there was more bad than good happening. In my heart I also wanted to re-create what I remembered as a child growing up in Germany, but from a logical standpoint, I knew that just wasn't going to happen.

Then, just before the holidays in 1973, Rick and I split up. I realized one sad day that it would be impossible to turn him around, and my goals as a family person had also failed. Back then I really wanted the marriage to work; I was dead serious that a marriage should be for life. I had two children with this guy, but I couldn't change him. The situation got more and more out of control, to the point where I had no choice but to end the insanity, and I literally threw him out of my house. Then I ended up having to sell my house to cut the ties.

I lost myself in my work during that time. I was almost never home, and my kids spent much more time with their babysitter than with me. I would go out on sales calls, I would take care of dogs, I was just always out doing something.

Miraculous Changes

One evening in February 1974, I had three appointments for Kirby that I had pre-screened, and they looked like easy sales. My babysitter, who was one of our neighborhood Christians, had taken my kids to church with her. It was a Wednesday night. My first appointment wasn't home, so I headed for the second appointment, but on the way there my car's headlights started blinking, and then they went out.

Where I live is pretty far out in the country, so headlights are something you really need at night. I cancelled my two appointments and headed home. The church was two blocks away from my road, so I decided, well, since I haven't had a chance to spend a lot of time with my boys lately, I'll just go pick them up and we'll spend a couple hours together.

The church was in a long, narrow building called First Bible Baptist. When I got there, the darned kids didn't want to leave. I argued with them, but they wanted to see the end of the movie that they were watching, so I said, okay, I'll wait twenty minutes. After twenty minutes, it was getting dark. I got my kids, and we got out to the car, but the lights didn't work. I knew that my babysitter was going to be going home after the service, and she lived across the street from me, so we decided to wait for her. But it was going to be an hour before the church let out.

I brought the kids back to the church's nursery, and the people there said, "Well, why don't you go upstairs and listen to the service?"

I said, "Oh jeez, that's all I want to do. I need to go outside and have a cigarette. I don't want to listen to the service." But it was cold. I didn't want to be standing outside in a snowstorm, smoking. So finally I said, "All right, I guess I'll go hear what this idiot's got to say up there."

So I went up and listened to what the idiot, a man named Peter Ruckman, had to say. I wasn't focused on him, or even actually watching him. I was just kind of listening. The sermon was about pride—about Satan's "I" trouble being what separated him from God. "I" will ascend. "I" will be like the most high—his pride caused him to lose God. The sermon went on and on, and everything he was saying made sense to me. For once in my life, I understood. I realized that I had a bad case of "I" pride, too.

Then all of a sudden a lady turned around from the seat in front of me and asked, "Are you saved?" She had a sweet Southern accent—an unusual thing to hear in upstate New York, and with a rush, it brought me back to good memories of traveling around the South with my dogs as a young girl. Right then and there I came unglued. I became mush. My pride slipped away, and on my knees, in the back of that church, with tears streaming down my face as Nancy Motley read verses to me, I asked Jesus to come into my life. I was saved on February 26, 1974.

The Shiloh Shepherd Is Born

After it was all over, I got my kids, and I totally forgot about the stupid headlights. I went out to the car, put the kids in, turned on the car, and the lights worked.

I drove all the way home with lights on, but the lights never worked again after that. I had to take it to the mechanic, and they told me I had a short circuit. Yeah, you can explain it, maybe, I had a short, I hit a bump, the car was moving, so starting it up the second time triggered something? Who knows. But after a while you look at that and say, you know, there's got to be something more to it.

That night after the service I came home and opened up the Bible, and I was amazed to find that it made perfect sense. I started reading it and understanding, just like you would read any book and understand it. After that I wanted to learn everything there was to know about the Bible: if you walk through a doorway, it's a good idea to find out as much as possible about what's behind that door. So I began to really study the Bible. I have not stopped studying it since.

Being a Christian is sometimes hard for me because people expect me to act a certain way. I still have a bit of a hardcore attitude on the outside. Every so often you'll hear me swear; every so often you'll see me reverting back to my youth, so to speak.

I'm not a goodie-two-shoes kind of Christian. But Christianity is a relationship with the Lord. I have no problem with that. I have a relationship with Jesus. It's a personal relationship. That night in 1974 was the beginning of a long road, full of lessons. I made a lot of changes in my life shortly after getting saved. Walking in that direction gave me peace in one way, but it was also a difficult walk.

It was around that time that I took Tammy to the training facility and watched her amazing performance as she switched gears in a heartbeat from attacking a decoy to being gentle with my two-year-old son. Any other dog would certainly have inflicted some damage on my toddler, but Tammy was able to stop herself in mid-attack. That was a defining moment in my career, but I was still hesitant to believe it at the time. Yes, I knew that Tammy was an incredible dog. But could I breed her to make more incredible dogs?

What I did next sounds terrible. I had accepted the Lord as my personal savior, but I wouldn't believe it unless I got a sign. I was like, okay, so if you're real, show me. Prove it. I had begun walking on God's path, but I was still a beginner.

One day I was reading the story of Hannah in my Bible. Hannah desperately wanted a child (she was barren), so she went to a place called Shiloh, to the house of the Lord, to petition him for a son. She promised the Lord that if he granted her desire, she would dedicate her son back to the Lord. I decided that I would do the same thing.

So I went out to my kennel and sat among my dogs, and petitioned the Lord to grant my dream. It was the 27th of April, 1974. I sat there looking at the problems that I had in some of my dogs, and the health issues that we were having, and I said, "Lord, I want to produce an animal that is worthy of being called a German Shepherd, that is like my grandmother's dogs used to be. A dog that is sound, that is stable, that is like Tammy! Lord, you give me those animals, and I will give you all the credit for them. If you're real, if you're really there, prove it. Give me the dog I want. Because I know for sure there is no human way to do it. It's impossible."

If God was really going to be my partner, I decided that the name Konigin kennels wouldn't fit. First of all, God is the king, and that kennel was named after the queen, so that didn't really work. Number two, Konigin Kennels wasn't doing so well, so I didn't see any point in beating a dead horse. I started thinking about a new name. I told the Lord, if we're going to go into this business together, if you're going to perform the miraculous and I'm going to do the grunt work, we've got to have a new name. The word Shiloh kept coming up; it is mentioned in the Bible thirty-three times. Genesis 49:10 says, "The scepter shall not depart from Judah, nor a lawgiver from between his feet, until Shiloh comes"—Shiloh refers to Jesus. It just felt right. *Shiloh Shepherd*.

I promised God that I would always acknowledge him as my partner in life, and the Shiloh Shepherd logo is designed to reflect that. The symbol of God's provision, the fish, is a testimony to Him. The nine stars in our club logo are symbolic as well. In the Bible, nine is the number of fruitfulness: There are nine fruits of the spirit in Galatians 5:22-23. There are nine gifts of the spirit in 1 Corinthians 12. It takes a woman nine months to produce a child (it takes a dog nine weeks!). The fish symbol and the nine stars have been associated with the Shiloh name for over three decades.

Nineteen seventy-four was a whirlwind year. It seemed like my head was spinning, but it was an exciting time. Within five months, Rick and I broke up, I realized where I wanted to go with the dogs, and then I made my pact with the Lord, and I renamed my kennel. From that day forward my dogs would be Shiloh Shepherds!

And then I waited to see what the Lord would do.

And of course, the Tammy puppies were phenomenal. That's the best litter that I've ever had, in forty years of breeding, and it became my foundation line for the Shiloh Shepherd. Every puppy in that litter was fantastic. I kept Shep, who was the biggest light gray sable. I trained most of those puppies myself, and they were amazing dogs.

Then, step by step, dog by dog, generation by generation, I saw my breeding program start to turn itself around. As I got to know these new dogs and their abilities, I realized that God really does answer prayers. The dogs were absolutely incredible.

Kennel logo

Chapter 3

Building a Firm Foundation

The Shiloh Shepherds Begin to Amaze

I felt the Lord's guidance helping me to find good dogs to bring into my breeding program, and one of the dogs I found soon after I renamed my kennels was Denni. Denni reminded me of my childhood friend Lady, who never could have pups, because all of my dogs were fixed when I was a kid. When Denni had a litter, I selected two females to keep. KariAnn was the smartest one, but Mitzie had the most show potential. I placed Mitzie with my mom, who had recently retired.

My mom had taken on a part-time job as a crossing guard for the local elementary school. She would often bring Mitzie to work with her. The kids just loved my mom (and Mitzie). But it wasn't long before I started hearing complaints from my mom—Mitzie was always trying to out-think her! This dog was smarter than any other she had ever had.

One morning my mom had a slight cold, and there was no school that day, so she thought she'd sleep in. Mitzie could not understand why my mom was not getting up, so she went into my mother's room and stuck her wet nose into her ear. That was not amusing, and my mom told her to get lost.

Not wanting to miss out on the fun of playing with the little children, Mitzie decided to be a little more persistent. There was a nightstand and a metal magazine rack between my mom's bed and the wall, so Mitzie went into the kitchen and got her stainless steel water dish, then returned with it in her mouth and started banging it as hard as she could against the metal rack. That got Mom out of bed fast, although not in the best of moods!

Mitzie was smart enough to push my mom around, and she was just the beginning.

Above: Mitzie with John.
Right: Anita's last Shiloh, Deeter, a KariAnn granddaughter.

In September of 1977 a little girl got lost in the Adirondacks, in a stretch of many miles of wilderness, not far from where I lived. Search teams were called in, but they couldn't find her. More search teams were added with more search dogs, but none of them could find the little girl. The girl's family was starting to panic. I was mopping the kitchen floor when the call came in, and I drove out to the scene with KariAnn, Mitzie's sister, who had been trained in search and rescue.

I was due to deliver a baby in seven weeks, so I started our searching on an easy grid, but KariAnn insisted on going up toward a very steep hill in another section. She refused to focus on our area. As it was going to be dark soon, I went back to the coffee camper and told Don, the team leader, what was happening. He refused to let me climb those slopes, due to my condition, and told me to rest my swollen ankles. He would take KariAnn up to where she wanted to go.

What happened, of course, was KariAnn found that little girl.

Once they found her, KariAnn and Don got all the glory, while pregnant me sat in a comfy chair elevating my feet. I hate to admit it, but I whined about missing out on that find for a long time. But I was unbelievably proud of my KariAnn! I was witnessing such an astounding change in my animals, every day was really exciting.

Little did I know that the next person one of my dogs would help would be me.

Lisa and Shep

My daughter Lisa was born with a heart defect. We had to do everything we could to keep her from crying and overexerting her heart. The doctors said she might outgrow some of her problems, but told us to be very careful because she could turn blue and not be able to breathe. She was what nowadays is called "SIDS potential."

Everybody in the house was always very careful around Lisa, making sure she didn't cry. The dogs, being smart animals, observed that if Lisa started crying, everybody immediately rushed to her, picked her up, and made her happy. Tammy's son, Shiloh-Emmview's Grey Express, whom we called "Shep," was one of our house dogs at the time. Apparently he had been observing things that we never realized he understood.

In the spring of 1978, I was returning from a dog show, one of many I traveled to in those days. It had been a very exhausting trip, and all I could think about was sleep. My babysitter was stressed out after three days of taking care of the kennel, the house, and the kids, and she just wanted to go home. Lisa was sound asleep. Shep, her guardian, was lying under her crib. Everything seemed normal, so I sent the sitter home and I fell asleep quickly.

A couple of hours later, Shep was on top of me, ripping my nightgown, going totally ballistic. My dogs never did that. He jumped off the bed and ran down the hall, ran back, jumped on me, ruff ruff ruff! He was whining so much, I thought I heard Lisa crying, but then I wasn't sure. Then I thought I heard her crying again. Then I didn't. I was so tired, I was certainly not thinking clearly. But Shep kept pulling at me and barking. He would not stop.

Tina with Lisa and Shep

Finally, he grabbed my nightgown in his teeth and proceeded to drag me down to the nursery. I looked in Lisa's crib and saw that she was turning blue! I picked her up immediately and ran downstairs to call an ambulance. They told me I was just in time to save her life.

That last cry that I'd thought I heard must have been Lisa's last before she went into convulsions; the doctors told me if I hadn't done anything, she would have died by morning. But thanks to Shep, I got to her in time, and she revived.

After that I knew that all my efforts in nearly twenty years of breeding dogs had been worth it. Shep was smart enough to know something was wrong, and he knew exactly what to do about it. I can still see the soul of Shep floating around in the eyes of so many Shilohs today: that degree of intelligence is actually what I expect from all my Shiloh Shepherds.

Getting It Right

I knew that I wanted KariAnn, my search and rescue dog, in my breeding program, so I started looking for a mate that was good enough for her. After a lot of thought, I decided to buy a dog named Max von Glendhenmere, Shaft of Delshire's son. He was the most expensive dog money could buy. Max was a gorgeous black and red male, one of the flashiest dogs in my kennel. He was also shown and champion pointed by my son. I was sure that he would be the ideal mate for KariAnn.

There was only one problem—she absolutely detested him. She refused to breed him! I tried and tried to get them together, but she always refused. Finally, I decided I was just going to make it happen. She was stubborn, but I was stubborn too. I asked several friends to come and help me. Since I knew we were in for a fight, we took the dogs into the barn, because it was softer with the straw in there, and the four of us tried to hold KariAnn down. We fought for hours that night, but she just wore us out; we were totally exhausted from just trying to hold her. KariAnn was not going to let Max mount her, so finally I told my friends, "Look, maybe she's not ready yet. Something's not right here, let's let her be. We'll try it again tomorrow morning. Maybe she'll have changed her mind."

We walked out of the barn with the dogs, and it was cold and damp out, and I was miserable. We put the two dogs back in the kennels, and I went to bed.

The next morning when I went out to the kennels, I couldn't believe my eyes. There was KariAnn, but she wasn't alone—a male dog was in her kennel with her. It was Shep, the same dog who had saved Lisa. Shep had climbed out of his own run, all the way on the other end of the kennel, and he had made it all the way around the building to get in with her. There they were together. And she seemed as happy as the cat that ate the canary.

I couldn't possibly breed KariAnn to Max at that point, so the only thing I could do was put Shep back in his own kennel, and then just leave them. I thought, "Oh well, we blew this heat! There's nothing I can do about it now." Because of all her search and rescue work, KariAnn hadn't had any puppies before, and she was getting older. I knew this might be her last chance. I could not believe that I had let it get so messed up.

Well, all this shows is that the Lord knows better than I do. KariAnn had ten wonderful puppies in that litter. One of those ten puppies was Shiloh's Kara Lobo of Emmview (Kari), who ended up being our foundation bitch and the preeminent dog in the Shiloh world.

***

Kari was a gorgeous dog with uncanny human-like intelligence, and the dogs from her line have always shared that same quality. Kari was everything Tammy had been, in super size! I was amazed to find that the Kari-line dogs had wonderful hips and no major health problems. I found that when I combined dogs from the Kari line with the old Wurttemberger Shepherd dogs, a type of farm shepherd that was also in the foundation lines used to establish the Leonberger and other breeds, I got a vast improvement of bone size and managed to keep all of the positive Kari traits.

But that was just the first of my pleasant surprises: I found that the Kari line would tone down the Ursa line's stubbornness. The Kari line washed out the Ria line's smaller size and ugly ears. It overpowered the Sabrina line's spookiness and health issues. As I kept crossing back into the Kari line, things really began to pull together.

Kari's background was very similar to that of London, the very famous dog from the "Littlest Hobo" movies, who could understand three languages, calculate arithmetic and even verbalize "hello." Kari always reminded me of London. Shiloh Shepherds have London in our gene pool too. Most of them can be trained to do the same things London did in his movies.

But of course, the most amazing thing of all was that the Kari line happened completely by accident. I didn't plan it, and I wouldn't have planned it; I wanted KariAnn to be bred to Max, not Shep. Thanks to that little miracle, the Shiloh Shepherd foundation was finally in place.

Kari's look alike great-granddaughter, dam of our G.V. Ch Zion-Chao's Spirit of Megan, Ch Ptd. Zion's Raven Out of the Mist (30 inch, Penn Hip excellent).

G.V. Ch Zion-Chao's Spirit of Megan

The following listing represents only some of the ROM descendents of an amazing dog, Shiloh's Kara Lobo of Emmview, that have made a giant impact on our entire breed. These Register of Merit descendents of Kari were also instrumental in producing so many of our other outstanding champions and ROM dogs bred by/born at Shiloh/Zion Kennels.

Title	Name	ROM Points
GV abCH	BIONIC BLACK SMOKE OF ZION	21980
GV abcCH	WINDSONG'S KATRINKA D'SHILOH	2945
GV bCH	SHILOH'S CAPTAIN-CALIBER BAKER	2945
GV NS brCH.	ZION'S A-TRIBUTE TO SNOWS GRIZZ	2520
GV bCH	PINEWOOD'S LIL-SHELBY OF ZION	1640
GV NS abiCH	ZION'S ENDEAVOR OF BETTER WAYS	1455
GV 4NS biCH	WILLAMETTE'S SISKIYOU'S CHAOS	1150
GV abCH	HILLTOP'S TRITON KING OF ZION	1075
NS abCH	KING ZEUS-OLYMPUS OF ZION	7670
NS abCH	SNOW'S A TRIBUTE TO PAX-ZION	5430
NS abcCH	PINEWOOD LAZARUS COMFORTH ZION	4945
NS abCH	SHILOH'S GRAND ELIZZABETH	2505
NS bCH	BETTERWAYS TRIBUTE TO SASQUACH	1355
NS abCH	SHILOH'S HANDSOME SAMSON	1145
NS abCH	MORIAH'S O DAUGHTER OF ZION	740
NS bCH.	ZION'S ANGUS QUINN FOR CASH	705
NS bCH	SIRIUS' DIVA OF BETTER WAYS	625
NS bCH	SHILOH'S TIMBER BLAZE	530
NS abCH	WINDSONG SHESHESHARONA OF ZION	505
NS bCH	SHILOH'S SAMPSON ZACHARY	400
NS abCH	LONDON SHOEN-HIRN VON ZION	320
NS bCH	ASGARD'S FREYIA OF BETTERWAYS	300
NS bCH	HIGHLANDERS RED SONJA OF ZION	295
iYOUTH SIEGER	VIC-MARS SISKIYOU SPIRIT	4715
abCH	BIONIC SNOW WARRIOR OF ZION	1180
abCH	SHILOH'S DEMURE DELILA	995
abCH	RICH HILLS CHELSA RAE OF ZION	320
abiCH	LADY'S ABBY OF BETTER WAYS	330
	SHILOH'S MATOAKA POCAHANTAS	9585
	SHILOH'S WOLFIN SASQUACH	8715
	ZION'S KELLCASTLE PITANNALEE	4715
	JNK SMOKE'N BLACK-BEAR OF ZION	505
	ZION'S THE MARK OF ZORRO	420
	K-SURA'S MISTIE WEATHER V ZION	2995
	VISION'S IRON MAIDEN	2355

MOUNTAIN SHEBA OF ZION	2260
ZION'S WINNIE-THE-POO	2120
WINDSONGS GYPSY DANCER OF ZION	2055
CRANE'S OUR-TRIBUTE-TO CONTESA	1905
ZION'S GRETCHEN STARR	1835
MOUNTAIN SNOW OF ZION	1765
FREESTATES STORM OF ZION	1620
ZION TAKES IT ALL	1615
SHILOH'S I OF-THE-TIGERS	1545
XENA WARRIOR PRINCESS OF ZION	1510
BETTER WAYS BELLE OF THE BALL	1455
JNK'S GOLDEN NUGGET OF ZION	1320
MONA'S LISA OF BETTER-WAYS	1260
ZION'S RUN FOR THE GOLD LADY	1170
ZION'S RAVEN OUT OF THE MIST	1150
JOAN'S NORTH STAR OF ZION	1025
PETRA'S ZENA OF ZION	1005
JNK'S MASTER TONKA BEAR	1000
MORIAH-ZION INDYPEN-DANCE DAWN	960
LONGOBARDI'S DOMINO OF ZION	950
ZION'S SILVER PRIMO BABY	925
THUNDER' N TORAH OF ZION	875
BRIGHT STAR OF BETTER WAYS	860
FISHER'S CISCO KID SPECTACULAR	740
SHENANDOAH'S DA SHEBA FOR ZION	690
ZION'S BIONIC-LONDON-SNOW	675
MAJESTIC SPIRIT OF ZION	625
SHILOH'S CELESTIAL CINNAMON	570
HIGHLANDERS GRAY-TOREY OF ZION	515
ZION-MISTY'S GOLDEN SABER	505
FREESTATES GIFT OF LOVE TO ZION	495
ZION'S WALKER-TEXAS RANGER	485
MONA'S LADY OF BETTER-WAYS	480
SHILOH'S DEAR ABBEY	475
GOLDEN ORCHA-KAYLA OF ZION	450
ZION'S RIPPIN RINNA	445
SHINING STAR OF VIC-MAR	440

LADY JESSICA OF ZION	400
SHILOH'S EASY RIDER	390
TRILLIUM-PETRA OUR AJAX D'LAZ	375
GOLIATH'S STEEL-SWORD OF ZION	360
ZION'S LAZ LIVES ON	350
ZION'S BLACK KING	340
ZION'S KNIGHT-RIDER-KIT	340
TRILLIUMS RED-HOT MUSTANG ZION	320
LIBERTY'S VENUS-OLYMPUS OF ZION	310
ZION'S GLORY FROM ABOVE SUKA	305
SHILOH'S STORM-N-SILVER WING'S	300
LIBERTY COCOA BELL OF ZION	280
ROARING ROCK'S JACOB OF ZION	280
SCHULER'S SASSY OF DA-JO	270
JNK'S SHAHARA ZOD	250

Please note: Dogs born at Shiloh Shepherds Kennel prior to the transformation still carried the "Shiloh" prefix. Later all of them carried "Zion." The other kennel names listed belonged to ISSR licensed breeders at the time the dogs were born.

A Time to Decide

Since January of 1975, we had been living in a beautiful new colonial outside of Hilton, New York. I had put a lot of time and money into remodeling the place to the specifications I needed for working with my dogs, but just when I got it up the way I needed it to be, people started buying the lots directly around me and building houses on them. Then one of my new neighbors complained about my dogs—evidently she was afraid of them. She started calling the police, trying to have me shut down.

I thought about moving farther out to the country, where I could have more space and fewer neighbors, but I had a good business going in town at the Kirby center, and I was teaching training classes throughout the week. If I moved, I would have to give all of that up. I would also lose that beautiful house, and all the money I had invested into making it workable for my dogs.

But if I stayed in that house, I would no longer be able to breed.

I didn't have to ponder the problem for too long. After Shep saved my baby Lisa, I knew in my heart that these dogs represented my mission in life. I sold the house at a loss and moved out to the country. With the Lord's guidance, I knew that this was the path I had to take.

The house I found was on Shearing Road in Gainesville, New York, right in the middle of nowhere. I bought the place very cheap; it was kind of a hunting cabin. There was no driveway, just an 1,800-foot-long tractor path leading from the bridge to the house. We put a driveway in, and it sank right away. I had to spend seven or eight thousand dollars a year after that just to keep the driveway up. But the driveway was only a small part of the problems with that property: our bridge had to be replaced constantly, the septic system had to be replaced, I re-built the barn, I built all the kennel units, the maternity ward, and a huge training center-office. Before I knew it I had put over a hundred and fifty thousand dollars into that place in improvements. All the money I had set aside was poured right into the expansion. The cost was astronomical.

I am not someone who does anything halfway. I decided that if I was going to leave my job and dedicate my professional life to the Shiloh Shepherds, then I was going to go full throttle. We moved in 1978, and I began expanding the kennel immediately. By the end of that year we had over a hundred dogs at our new home.

Now let me make one thing very clear: I've never wanted to be a millionaire. When people talk to me about breeding dogs and they've got big dollar

Summer view: Lisa on driveway

signs in their eyes, I know their hearts are not in the right place. What does appeal to me is having the money to do what I want to do with the dogs, and in that regard, I hate to be limited. If there's a dog I want for the gene pool and it's going to cost me forty thousand dollars, and I can't buy him but I really need him, that is painful! But if I had forty thousand dollars would I want to go out and buy a fancy car? No. That's just not me.

There's a lot of financial stress in what I do. Unless you're selling puppies for three or four thousand dollars, you really don't make money. In today's market, health testing alone can cost up to a thousand dollars—on just one dog! Just the basic kibble for one dog runs thirty to forty dollars per month. If

Bird's Eye View of some of the Shiloh Farm

The property consists of 3 separate pastures with heated barn, house and 6 whelping rooms in new heated building. It is designed to easily accomodate over 50 dogs.

from Shiloh Shepherds Newsletter

you add meat and supplements, not to mention regular wormers, boosters, etc., you should expect to spend well over a thousand dollars per dog, per year! So now you've got about two thousand dollars invested in one dog until it reaches breeding age, and that's if the dog does not have any health problems. And that doesn't include the original value of the pup. Then there is the necessity of placing stock that does not meet the breeding requirements (for example, if they fail any of their tests), not to mention unforeseeable expenses resulting from unexpected health or accident issues.

You've got to invest so much into your potential breeding stock, there's really no reason to breed dogs unless you love what you're doing. It's unbelievably expensive if you do it right—and of course, I have always tried to do it right.

So as prices for my Shiloh Shepherds steadily grew, my expenses grew right along with them.

My advertising bill back then ran well over a thousand dollars a month. I was making sure the Shiloh Shepherds were in all the important newspapers, dog magazines, in the ROBB report, an elite millionaire's magazine, and even on radio commercials. My accountant never ceased to be amazed when I brought in my boxes full of receipts for those long tax returns! At the same time I was increasing production to keep up with the demand, I was writing articles for major dog magazines, I was going to dog shows, and I was expanding my kennels to accommodate well over a hundred dogs. It was exhausting. In hindsight I'm not sure how I ever did it.

What kept me going was the undeniable fact that the Shiloh Shepherds were making progress. Madame Curie spent all of her life trying to discover radioactivity, and I'm sure that wasn't an easy life! It was only after she accomplished her mission that everybody congratulated her. It's the same way for anybody who is trying to use his or her life to obtain a difficult goal. I had to do a lot of hard work along the way without much help. It was never easy.

But the dogs were improving, and it was a delight to watch my children grow up alongside such magnificent creatures. And as the dogs improved, so did my reputation: to my surprise, I found that I'd become a sought-after expert on dog genetics.

Dog World *ad from the '80s*

Common Sense Seminars

I never took any courses in genetics, but once I started making progress on canine hip dysplasia, I was a self-made celebrity. People started calling me with questions, or asking me to come speak to their dog clubs. It didn't matter to them that I was not experienced at professorial levels. I don't know a single thing about Mendel's pea plants. But I do understand genetics, and I also understand dog breeders.

Scientists had figured out the science of genetics, but I was able to present the information in a way that made sense to breeders, and that was revolutionary. The general breeder doesn't want to hear about Mendelian theory and peas and pods. What they want to know is, Why are we getting plush-coated puppies, when both the parents have smooth coats?

The first thing that I introduced in my practical genetics seminars was the shadow dog concept: What you see is not what you're going to get! I would ask breeders in my classes, "What does your dog's shadow dog look like?" People would say, "Shadow dog? Well, I don't know."

I'd tell them straight away, you shouldn't be breeding anything if you don't know what your shadow dog looks like, because that's what you're going to produce in your puppies. A shadow dog represents all of the recessive traits your dog is carrying. Many of the breeders who went to my seminars were still breeding dogs from famous lines to other dogs from famous lines, with no inkling about pedigree research. This was a whole different perspective on breeding for them: I told them, you've got to have some idea of what the possibilities are before you breed two dogs, I don't care how famous those two dogs happen to be.

So what does the Shadow Dog look like? In order to find out, you need to understand my theory of crayons and boxcars.

Genetic Inheritance Made Simple

Genetic inheritance is a pretty complex concept, so I made up an analogy that drastically simplifies it. Picture chromosomes as boxcars on a train. Each boxcar carries a single row of multicolored crayons. The crayons inside the boxcars represent genes, which are responsible for the final characteristics of the puppy, both good and bad.

The crayons (genes) from the stud arrive in the dam in a single line of boxcars (chromosomes). At that time, they pair up with the dam's corresponding line of boxcars and form a double line. Inside the cars, a crayon from one parent corresponds to a crayon from the other parent, thus forming a large number of crayon pairs. Each gene, or pair of crayons, is responsible for a certain characteristic of the puppy (coat color, height, etc), which makes up the dog's physical appearance, or phenotype.

Imagine that you take the crayons out of a boxcar pair and hold them in your hand. Now you find another complication: the crayons come in two sizes—long and short! And they come in a rainbow of colors! The dog's phenotype of discernable characteristics, as well as the "shadow dog" characteristics that you won't see, are determined by the makeup of the crayon pairs. The long crayons represent dominant characteristics, and the short crayons represent recessive characteristics.

If a pair is made up of two longs, or dominants, they will be crayons of the same color, and the puppy will exhibit the characteristics of a long crayon. If the pair is made up of two short crayons, or recessives, they will also be crayons of the same color, and the puppy will exhibit the recessive characteristic. The fun starts when the puppy inherits a short crayon from one parent and a long crayon from the other. In a pair with one long and one short, the crayons will always be different colors.

Contrary to popular wisdom, a puppy with a dominant/recessive pairing for a characteristic will most likely *not* show a characteristic that is between the "long" and the "short" crayon. For example, an aggressive dog bred to a coward will not produce a "medium" temperament. The resulting puppy might display his inherited cowardly (dominant) characteristics, but when bred to a "soft" dog that also has an inherited recessive (shadow) for aggression, it will in all probability produce some uncontrollably aggressive progeny.

In dominant/recessive pairings, the dog will display the dominant characteristic—the long crayon—but it still will be carrying the short crayon, which is riding along unnoticed on its train of chromosomes.

Let's imagine a fictitious gene, or crayon pair, that controls whether a puppy is born with four legs or three legs. Say the long crayon in this particular pair is blue, and the short one is green. We will have three possible genetic combinations (genotypes): blue/blue, green/green, and green/blue. But there are only two possible physical appearances (phenotypes): dogs with four legs, and dogs with three legs.

A combination of two long blue crayons produces a puppy with four legs.

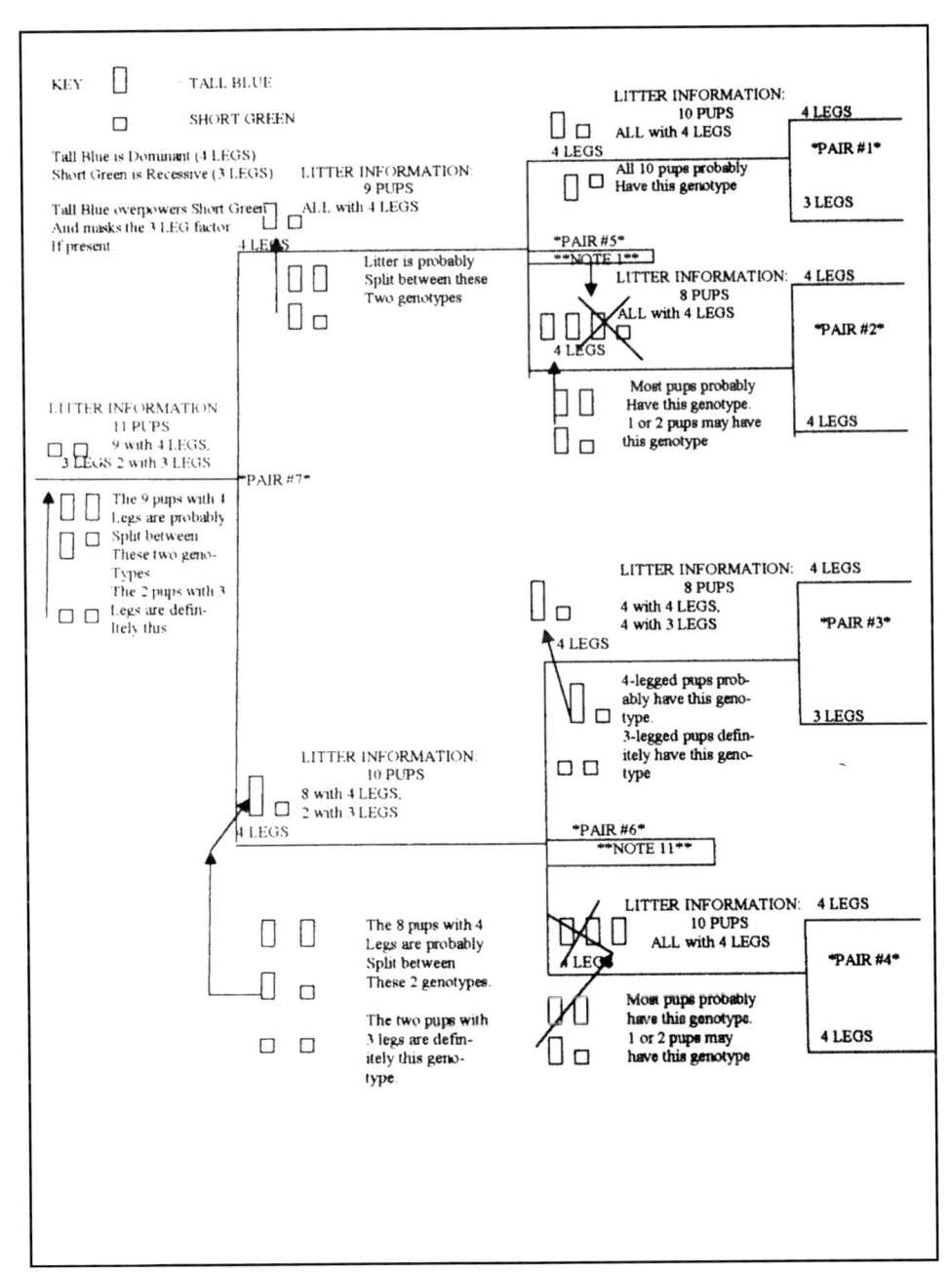

Chart from Genetics Seminar/article

A pair of short greens produces a puppy with three legs. In the pair consisting of one long blue crayon and one short green crayon, the blue crayon is dominant. That puppy will have four legs, exactly like the puppy with the "pure" combination of two blue crayons. But he is carrying a recessive gene.

The dog with the mixed short crayon/long crayon (dominant/recessive) gene appears absolutely normal. But when that dog becomes a parent, he will contribute half of his genetic makeup to the next generation, and there's a 50-50 chance he will pass that short green crayon on to his offspring. If his mate also has a recessive short green crayon, this greatly increases the chance of producing three-legged puppies!

A breeder's best bet is the dog with two blue crayons. He will pass one or the other of those blue crayons on to future generations. Since the blue crayon is dominant, all future pups will have four legs. Even if by some chance they inherit a short green crayon from the other parent, the puppies will always be safe from that defect.

That is my breeding secret—it's not complicated. The "two blue crayon" dog is a good dog to keep in your breeding program; get as many of those as you can for the characteristics you're trying to lock in. If you rely on dogs with dominant good characteristics, you can stack your deck—remove most of the number cards in your breeding program, and replace them with queens, kings, jacks and aces. Do that, and you're much more likely to win the game!

My students would say, "Okay, but how do I find which dogs are carrying two dominant genes, and which are carrying recessives?"

Good question. Even the most advanced geneticists in the world can't look at a dog and tell us that. All a breeder can do is find out as much as possible about the history of their dog's entire gene pool, and go from there. Survey littermates, aunts, uncles, cousins—any recessive trait that you see represented in your dog's ancestors is probably carried by your shadow dog, and it should be noted. That is why my LMX system has been so successful. By tracking the littermates, we can unveil the recessives that could become problematic in future generations.

If you are able to find dogs that have "clean" pedigrees for five or six generations for whatever you're trying to breed out—hip dysplasia, for example—then you can be pretty sure you're looking at dogs with two dominants, or long crayons, for that gene.

And that, in a nutshell, is how I dramatically reduced the hip dysplasia problem in the Shiloh Shepherd.

***

When I talked about breeding out canine hip dysplasia, I had a captive audience amongst German Shepherd breeders, who were increasingly obsessed with that problem. But they weren't the only ones interested: The Labrador, Golden Retriever, Doberman Pincher, Rottweiler, and even the Australian Cattle Dog were all starting to display some hip problems, and their clubs got in touch with me too.

Every time I gave my talk to a group of future breeders, someone would say, "I'd like to invite you to another club, so you can share this with some of the other breeders there." I'd agree, and before I knew it I was flying all over the country doing genetics seminars. I went to just about every state in the nation. I talked to the Great Dane, Doberman and Rottweiler clubs; I went from coast to coast across North America from Halifax, Nova Scotia to Victoria, British Columbia and from Orlando to Jackson Hole, Wyoming. By the late '70s I was writing articles for many of the breed newsletters and other publications, including the *German Shepherd Quarterly*.

In the early '80s I went to the Albany, New York, area a few times to conduct seminars for the monks of New Skete and their German Shepherd breeding program there. I remember that after my lecture, the monks ran around putting pedigrees on all the blackboards—if this one breeds to this one, they get funky tails, if this one breeds to this one, we get donkey ears—they were having fun with my genetic seminars. I was having fun too, flying around the country educating people.

But as I worked hard to get good breeders going in the right direction, I noticed that some breeders were going the other way.

Monks of New Skete Seminars

Puppy Mills

Once I got my "formula" right, the popularity of my Shiloh Shepherds skyrocketed. I was selling my dogs for thousands of dollars, and the demand was already outpacing my supply. That's when I started to come across unscrupulous breeders who were attempting to make a quick profit by exploiting the name I had chosen for the breed.

Those "breeders" would often purchase a pet-quality pup from me, and then would proceed to go on a breeding frenzy with the poor dog. They would keep a few of the biggest pups from each litter, and just keep producing more "pet quality" pups. Ads like, "AKC German Shepherd pups, Giant Shiloh bloodlines, reasonably priced," became popular.

It was depressing. It was also frustrating, because there was so little I could do to stop them. A lesson that I learned over and over is that people who just want to make money on dogs don't have the heart of a real breeder.

The more popular my dogs became, the more I encountered bad breeders who were making decisions for the sake of money, and didn't care about what happened to any of their pups further down the road. They didn't care if a poor creature from their gene pool had to spend his life tied out on a chain, or if he ended up in a dog shelter. They were only after the money.

Dog World *ad; last Shiloh Shepherds Kennel ad—1991*

Why did I care what these so-called "breeders" were doing? Aside from my obvious dismay at this abusive treatment of animals, it was also true that the Shiloh Shepherd was only as good as its reputation. If my dogs had a reputation for intelligence, size, and good hips, people would pay a lot of money for the dogs. But if people bought a German Shepherd from a puppy mill that was advertised as being "Shiloh bloodlines," and it did not have these characteristics, the reputation I'd worked so hard for could, I realized, be seriously damaged.

My war with the puppy mills would last for the next ten years, and it never ceased to make me furious. It was like a war against drunk drivers. I figured, if enough people screamed loudly enough, something would change! But, as I continued to learn throughout the highs and lows of my dog career, unscrupulous breeders never go away. If anything, as prices for Shilohs continued to rise, the bad breeders got meaner and meaner, and the battles I had to fight got tougher.

Ursa—Another Life-Saving Shiloh

Ursa was one of my foundation dogs, and her Ursa/Gunsmoke progeny continued her legacy for many generations. Every time I repeated that pairing I got amazing results. That pairing is partially responsible for the good hips of the Shiloh Shepherd breed. One of her progeny, Luke, is pictured in our club logo. Another of her progeny, Shiloh's Our Image of Ursa, who we also called "Ursa," was my son John's best friend.

One fateful winter day, my oldest boy Richard pulled his sled home with what looked like their Ursa's lifeless body in it. I ran out to meet him, yelling "What happened?" The boys had been sliding around on the frozen pond in the back pasture, something they were not supposed to be doing. Somehow, things had gone very wrong.

Did Ursa try to warn them that they should stay closer to the edge? Or did she try to push her best friend back toward safety? I guess we will never know what really happened. All I know is that it was Ursa who fell through the ice, not her friend, my six-year-old son Johnny.

All Richie told me was that he somehow managed to pull Ursa out, but she did get a lot of water into her lungs. Johnny was sitting in the sled holding the wet and freezing dog. I didn't think she was going to make it. He begged me to save her, but I didn't know if I could. We got her into the whelping box and turned on the heating pads and heat lamps that we use for newborn pups. I didn't know what else to do, so I told the boys to pray.

My son wanted to sleep with her, but I told him that she would be fine. I didn't think that was true; however, I couldn't stand the thought of her dying next to him during the night.

The next morning Johnny wouldn't go to school because he was so worried. He came with me to take Ursa to the vet. When I entered the maternity ward I expected the worst, but as soon as she saw Johnny she sat up and wagged her tail. By some miracle, she was a little bit better. The vet gave her some antibiotics to prevent a respiratory infection, and told us that it could still go either way. In the end Ursa survived. To this day I think that Ursa would have given her life for my son. I also believe that it was his love that saved her.

Chapter 4

Challenge and Change

Epidemic

The summer of 1980, I had a huge, gorgeous black and red male dog named Brutus, that I took to a local show to get his C.D. title. Brutus was just a year old. When we got back from the show, he had severe diarrhea, and by the next day he had started vomiting.

It didn't worry me much; I figured it was stress from the show. The next day Brutus was dehydrated, and he still wasn't eating, and we decided maybe we should put him on some fluids. I still wasn't too concerned, but I did notice that the smell from his stool was weird, like nothing I had ever smelled before. The next day he died. Within forty-eight hours of the time he got sick, Brutus was dead.

They tested him at the vet clinic and found that he had Parvo virus. This was before most breeders even knew what Parvo virus was. I was in no way prepared for it.

Since I didn't know anything about Parvo, while Brutus was sick I had been going back and forth in my kennels and walking around my puppies. Well, within two or three days, all my litters started to come down sick. Then one by one, they started dying too.

Then, in what seemed like an instant, all the dogs were sick. We were working around the clock putting fluids into them, trying desperately to keep them alive. I had puppies on my kitchen table hooked up to IV's; I had puppies in my bathroom in the tub on IV's, puppies hooked up everywhere. My family and I were up night and day, doing anything we could to save those dogs. We had fifty-two puppies on the property at the time, and we lost thirty-eight. And I was one of the lucky ones. Most kennels that got Parvo lost every single dog they had.

There's a lot of heartbreak involved in dog breeding, and I thought I was prepared to handle it, but that Parvo virus was almost more than I could take. Things had been riding high, and everything was looking phenomenal, and then it crashed and burned so quickly. I lost nearly all of what I cared about most. An epidemic like that is like dealing with the Black Plague or a natural disaster, like a tornado or a flood; it just happens. The odds of having to deal with several major disasters in your lifetime are much higher if you choose to breed dogs for a living. Parvo took me down a big hill, and it took me a very long time to build back up, both financially and emotionally.

Once we were finally through it, I realized that I needed to clean house. I had to take a deep breath and look at what I had left. When I worked up my nerve to take stock, I realized how much of my genepool I had lost. That was the very worst moment for me. I remember I closed my eyes, and I tried to understand that the Lord had a reason. I didn't know what it was, but I just told myself to keep moving forward. That was all I could do.

Shearing Road—Full Force

After the Parvo crisis, I forced myself to rebuild again, and threw myself into the breeding program with every ounce of energy I had. On May 2, 1982, Gary and I got married. That was when I really started working around the clock. I had three, four, or five litters at a time in the kennels, and I hired several employees to help me.

Tina with her husband, Gary Levesque, her parents, and her children: Richard, Lisa and John.

Taking care of a hundred dogs is an enormous amount of work—one person could never do it. I had rotation crews: The day crew came from eight o'clock until one or two in the afternoon; in the afternoons I had decoys coming in for training; and then I had a night crew that came in from four until eleven at night. Groomers came in three days a week, and they rotated through the dogs, grooming three or four dogs a day. I hired a secretary, and she cleaned and fed the puppies in the morning. My payroll alone was over two thousand dollars a month.

Even when I had 136 dogs in my kennel, five full time employees, and people working around the clock, it was still not enough for me. I needed to expand even more, so my experimenting could go faster! By the mid-80s, I started many "satellite" kennels breeding under my full supervision, so that there would be more data I could collect for the LMX program.

In the beginning I would give satellite breeders some of my dogs, and then buy the pups back from them at a reduced price. This worked fine with the people who took good care of the pups, but eventually I began to run into folks who would skimp on the prenatal and early puppy care in order to save on expenses. Wormy, malnourished puppies can be prone to developing environmentally-induced health issues as they mature, due to a compromised immune system. It was a heavy financial burden on my shoulders to bring them back to peak condition; not to mention the potential damage to the LMX program from badly-raised puppies. By the late '80s I had started to deal more in co-ownerships instead of simple fosters—people took better care of their puppies if they had more at stake.

Managing my operations, my satellite breeders, my employees, and my training business was no easy thing. To keep organized, I had my office in the training center built like a kitchen. I had bookshelves on one end, and a desk—the rest was ringed with cabinets on top and on the bottom. It was a huge building, and chock full of data. I was starting to amass quite a collection of LMX data. I had started linking my prices for puppies to how many generations back I had LMX information. So the more data I kept, the more money the puppies were worth.

My LMX program was beginning to get quite a good reputation in America as well as overseas. Many Europeans took an interest in what I was doing; there is a program that is mandatory now in Europe that looks very much like LMX.

Meanwhile, my monthly advertising budget skyrocketed to almost four thousand dollars. Month after month, year after year, the public kept hearing "Shiloh is the giant version of the German Shepherd: If you want a stable, super-sized companion that has good hips, and can be trusted with your children—you need a Shiloh!" I was advertising in *Dog World* and *Dog Fancy* that my dogs were 98% hip dysplasia free, and I'd prove it.

We mailed out large information packets at a rate of two to three dozen packets a day, each with twenty to thirty pictures of my dogs in them. In the late '70s I started passing out a small version of my stock book, listing the dogs I had in the kennel, with pictures and a little bit of information about each. In 1985 I enlarged this, and in '86-'87 we did a twenty-eight-page edition and mailed out thousands of copies. I also sent out over 5,000 color picture collages during the early '80s in order to promote my Shiloh Shepherds.

People were constantly calling with inquiries for more information about the breed. I spent four or five hours on the phone every day, talking to customers and answering questions. People would ask, "Why should I pay you three times more for a puppy?" and I'd say, "You're going to pay, honey. But you can pay now, or pay later. You can pay me $900 for this puppy, or you can pay somebody else $300 for a puppy and spend a thousand on vet bills, if you'd rather do a hip replacement or some other medical procedure. Which would you rather do?"

After examining the facts, they usually bought a Shiloh Shepherd.

I tried to sneak in an hour a day to read my Bible, and an hour or two to play with my horses, but aside from that I worked from seven in the morning till midnight, continuously dealing with all kinds of dog issues. My life was running at the pace of a flat-out sprint. Until one day, something hit me that I never saw coming.

Cancer

I had been having a lot of trouble with my menstrual cycles for a while, but I didn't tell anyone about it. I had massive bleeding, enough that it was starting to scare me. But I ignored it and just went on as usual. Then one day, I was carrying two thirty-pound buckets of mush across from the training center out to the kennels. As I went by the barn, I started hemorrhaging, and I fell to the ground. My son ran up and saw that my pants were pure blood. I passed out, and both of my boys dragged me into the car and drove me to the Gainesville fire department. At the fire department I could vaguely hear my son hitting the buzzer and yelling "Something's wrong with Mom, she's in the back seat, bleeding!"

The EMTs took me to the hospital, and the doctors there decided not to let me out. They said I had endometrial cancer.

I was in the hospital for a few days while they did some tests, and then they sent me to Roswell, where they did a complete hysterectomy. I didn't take well to being sick: within two weeks I was back home and at work again. They had me on chemotherapy for a while, and they put me on some strange pills that I had a lot of trouble with, and I didn't exactly take those pills as much as I was supposed to. I got a little bit better, but then I got worse because I wasn't taking my medication right. I ended up back in the hospital. That was just before Homecoming in 1984. I was so upset, because all I wanted to do was to go to Homecoming.

It was scary to be diagnosed with cancer, but I knew that if the Lord wanted me to be here, then I would be here. I don't remember feeling scared about dying—I mean, there have been many times that I felt I would have been better off dead. Sometimes I felt like, Let me out of here, I'm tired of this! Too much work! Too much responsibility! But at that point, I guess I knew that God wanted me to stick around. And I did beat the cancer. It's been in remission for over twenty years now.

The day before Homecoming, the biggest day of my year, when all my dogs and their owners came to my house for a huge party, I was still in the hospital in Warsaw, New York. So I told my doctor he had a choice of one of two things. I said, "You can either look out that window and watch me walking down Main Street in Warsaw, pulling this IV bottle, while wearing this funky little gown with my butt sticking out, hitchhiking, or you can let me out of here." So he let me out for Homecoming.

My children and I always tried to participate in the annual Caravan for Cancer that started out from our local park in Gainesville, New York, and traveled the nine miles (including down Shearing Road) all the way to the Pike Fairgrounds. Although I tried to take pictures of each event, most have been lost due to the fire, but since this was one of the few family activities that was extremely important to us, I am glad that my mom chose to keep a few of these pictures in her family album.

Lisa and Tina on horses at fair.

Richard and Lisa get in line at the park.

Heading to the park.

A Special Homecoming

By the early '80s Homecoming had turned into quite an event. We held it in my twelve-acre pasture, complete with tents, port-a-potties, Schutzhund demonstrations, temperament tests, shows, games, big bands, and food. We invited guest speakers and held seminars. I remember roasting marshmallows around a big bonfire, talking about dogs. People laughed, danced, talked... I had a chance to see my litters together in one place, so I could document more data for the LMX program, and people had a chance to have a lot of fun. There were consistently between eighty-five to a hundred and fifty people at Homecoming throughout the '80s.

I had to go to Homecoming that year in a wheelchair, but it ended up being one of the best days of my life. Gary, my husband at the time, and my son Richard got a hold of a lot of people who had been important in my life, and invited them to Homecoming: George Theriot, the man who started the National Schutzhund Association in America; Fred Lanting, my hip mentor; Gerhardt Sieger, my Schutzhund mentor; Mary Belle Adelman, a great breeder and one of the foremost women in Schutzhund... They were all there. Everybody.

It was an extended family reunion of the greats of great times. George Theriot personally awarded me the NASA medal of recognition for most dedicated service to the Schutzhund sport. Gerhart brought the whole Schutzhund club down there and did a fantastic demo for all my customers. Fred Lanting judged a show; everybody was there. I guess they figured that if the cancer returned, this could be my last reunion, and they wanted to make sure it was memorable. But actually the reunion inspired me to get better quickly. Maybe that's why I did.

SHILOH HOMECOMING 1984

"Shiloh Homecoming 1984"

Lisa "Puppy-sitting"

This is SCHUTZHUND!

Jackie and Lance

Zdenek with his Avalanche dog Timbe Try out Schutzhund!

Puppy evaluation

What's next Mom?

Get him!

Some NASA members get together

Peter points the way

What are we waiting for?

Gary and Cisco

Mass Confusion

Joe spots the decoy!

Come on Mom - we can't miss the Homecoming!

10 mo. old Cuyo meets his brother!

My Kids Learn the Trade

Richie, Johnny and Lisa didn't exactly have "normal" childhoods. We didn't do regular things, like take vacations or go to Disneyland, but they did get to spend a lot of time with animals. My kids were my business partners, in a sense, right from the beginning. I advertised that my dogs were all raised with kids, and that was part of the reason I could guarantee great temperaments. I grew up watching what my father did, and I began showing my kids, at a very young age, how to train dogs. They all have a talent for working with animals.

I was involved with various men throughout the years, but those relationships were not as important to me as my kids or my career. Most of those men were good decoys—they were good with the dogs, which was really the main key. They liked dogs, they just didn't know what they were doing, and eventually we would always run into conflicts. My kids were much more reliable than the men in my life.

When Lisa was twelve years old I decided to throw her into the deep water of the dog world, and I took her along to steward for me at one of the shows I was judging. A steward is a judge's assistant, but one that's supposed to know more than the judge, in the way a secretary sometimes knows more about proper procedure than the executive. Judges often bring their own stewards; husband-and-wife teams sometimes work together. I had never seen a twelve-year-old steward before, but I still knew that Lisa was the one I wanted for the job.

The problem was, Lisa had never been to a real, premier dog show before. She definitely didn't know how to be a steward. So all the way to Maryland in the car, a nine-hour drive, I explained to her what she needed to do. All the formalities and the rules and the regulations of dog shows make for quite a lot of information. I know people who have been showing dogs for years that don't know all those things. So it was a crash course, and we went over and over everything a hundred times.

As we were driving I said things like: "Okay, Lisa, when people come in with their entries, and they say, 'What class do I enter this dog?' what is your answer?" And she would say, "Well, the first thing I ask is, has this dog been shown before?"

She was getting all the right answers, but all the way down there, I was still sweating. I was thinking, I hope she can handle this, I hope I did the right thing by bringing her! But I told her, "Don't worry about it, Lisa, while you're at the steward's table I'll kind of sneak in, and if I hear something going wrong, I'll poke you with my elbow and say, 'Oh, that dog ought to be in such and such,' and I'll make sure that you don't screw up." We had a plan. But I was still pretty nervous.

Some AKC people can be snobbish. I've lived with them, these are my people, so I understand that this is normal, and it has never really bothered me. But of course the first person we ran into at the show was an older lady, she was an FCI judge, and quite a British snob. We got over to ringside, and she said, "Who did they assign to you for a steward?" and I said, "Well, they didn't, I brought my own." And she looked at my daughter and said, in a really prissy way, "That child is not your steward!"—as if the thought of such a thing happening at her prestigious TOBI show was incomprehensible.

Some people do things just by the book, and don't ever step aside from the book, and she was one of those people. I was going to be judging at "The" TOBI matches, an extremely elite rare breed show. I could understand why the idea of a twelve-year-old steward unsettled her.

But I stood my ground. I said, "Yes, this is my daughter, and she's quite capable of handling the job."

The woman was really upset; she was going on and on about how there were going to be camera people there from the local TV channels, and magazine writers, and world-renowned photographers... and famous authors like Bruce Fogle. I was thinking, great. I didn't know any of that until we got there. Nothing like putting a little stress on a person!

I just looked at the judge and said, "I'm very comfortable with my daughter, and she's been doing this for quite a long time." She said, "Well! If I had known this was going to happen—but you're starting in fifteen minutes! You'd better set up!"

During the judging the lady kept coming back, spying on us, making sure that everything was going right. But Lisa never missed a beat. She was right on target every step of the way. She did a perfect job, it was like we danced through the whole thing. A lot of times judges will stop, or they'll make notes, or they'll have to whisper to their steward, and it distracts from the whole flow of the show. But Lisa and I went like a clock, like we'd been doing that all of our lives.

When that show was over, the lady walked up to Lisa and she patted her on the back and said, "I like the way you run your procedures. You have a marvelous future. I hope you continue with dogs, because you're a natural."

That was when I knew that Lisa should take over with my Shiloh Shepherds if anything ever happened to me. After my cancer there was always a cloud: what if the cancer came back? It seemed like a good idea to get Lisa ready to step forward.

Lisa and Megan.

Personal Protection

Way back in the '60s, when I first started out, I got breeding stock in trade for some of my handling services, and I would train a few of my dogs to sell as personal protection dogs. I kept doing this throughout the years, and by the '80s, my personal protection dogs had gained such a reputation for excellence that they were selling for twelve to sixteen thousand dollars each. This was always a side-business for me, and it helped to support the costs of breeding.

I trained my personal protection dogs to do most of what Schutzhund dogs did, and then some, with the exception of the tracking and dumbbell work, which was time-consuming and not very useful. Dogs that had been put through my intensive training were extremely easy to handle. All the buyers I sold to were wealthy, and mostly they were women. They didn't want to have a gun in the house, and they didn't want to buy a Schutzhund dog, because it was almost impossible for a woman, and even some men, to handle a Schutzhund dog. And some of those dogs were not trustworthy around children. But a well-trained Shiloh Shepherd—that was another story!

Basically, I trained my personal protection dogs to be highly-skilled BS artists. Instead of biting the guy because "I want to kill the sucker!" they were playing with him, the way they would with a ball. Sort of like shadow boxing. My analogy was that putting one of these dogs on a "fass" command was like pulling out a .357 Magnum *water pistol*. Very impressive, but 100% safe! They were not trained to kill anyone; they were just trained to put on a heck of a good act. That way, they would never hurt the mailman, the milkman, the gas and electric guy checking your meter, or the teenager who throws his ball into your yard. After all, the chances of somebody breaking into your house to kill you are much slimmer than somebody coming into your house for some other reason. But the dogs could put on enough of an act to scare off the burglar if one should try to break in. And that's why they were going for so much money.

I remember one client in particular named Don. I always spent three days with each client, teaching them how to handle their new dog properly, because what's the good of having a dog if you don't know how to use it?

On this occasion Don and I got out of the car, the dog came out too, and we walked up to a Seven Eleven. I told the dog, whose name was Turk, "*platz*" (stay) and opened the door to go into the store. Don said, "With all these cars around, is he going to be okay?" I said, "Oh, yeah, don't worry about it."

So we went into the store and got some coffee and talked for a while. When we came out of the store, the dog was right where I had left him. He hadn't budged. We started walking away, and I said "heel," and the dog was automatically in heel position—no leash or anything. I could tell that Don was impressed. As we passed a flower shop he asked me if I could get Turk to "*platz*" again, and I did. Then we walked in to the flower shop and he asked me what kind of roses I liked. I told him I liked yellow, and he bought every yellow rose and pink carnation they had in the store! He presented them to me and said he'd never seen anybody train a dog like that before.

Schutzhund training.

KILLER at 1 year ready for action!!

The Shiloh Shepherds that I trained in personal protection were selling for huge amounts of money, and people didn't blink an eye to pay it, if it meant they were getting a dog that could do those things. But for me, the funny thing has always been that in Europe, all the dogs do that. You take dogs into restaurants. You take dogs into stores. The dogs are better behaved in Europe than some children are in America. In Europe, you carry your purse, you have your dog. It's what everybody does.

Throughout the '80s, as my breeding continued, and as the dogs I trained in personal protection sold for more and more money, I noticed that something about my dogs was different: They were getting easier and easier to train. At first I thought it was a coincidence, but as it continued to happen, I realized that it must be because of their breeding. The Shiloh Shepherd dogs were really getting smarter and stronger with every generation.

Dogs Are Changing

I never intended to "change" the breed. My early goals were to preserve the type of German Shepherd dog that I was so in love with, the kind that I remembered from my childhood. But by the '80s the average Shiloh puppy was already quite distinguishable from the rest of the German Shepherd crowd. They were much bigger, they didn't have the German Shepherd angulation; they were smarter and more stable; they were noticeably different. One day it dawned on me that if the Shilohs kept developing the way they were, one day they wouldn't be German Shepherds at all.

I kept breeding, and experimenting, and thinking a lot about how the dogs were changing. With 136 dogs in the breeding program, I could finally test all my theories out. I bred lots of experimental litters in order to collect data on my chosen bloodlines, and I bred dogs from my selected lines together to ascertain the compatibility of certain combinations.

The basic three lines that I was very happy with were Ursa, Ria, and Kari. Kari, of course, was my number one, super-intelligent, ideal Shiloh, although a lot of her progeny were tall and leggy, as well as bitchy-headed. The Ursa line gave us bulk, more consistency, the old-type look, but they were a little more stubborn, and hard-headed. With the Ria line I lost some leg, but I got stockier dogs with broad heads, even if some had soft backs and oversized ears. Every line had its faults! So I would take the bitchy-headed Kari and put it with the broad-headed Ria, and voila!

Then I would work hard to select the best specimens for the next generation. Some of the puppies took after one parent or the other, and of course some had all the faults of both. But some had all the virtues of both lines, and those were the ones that I pulled out, and I put them in the breeding program for the next generation. Having so many dogs allowed me to experiment all the time, and to slowly get closer to perfection.

Of course, by this point in my career I knew that breeding is largely trial and error. Even when I did all the calculations, and all the predictions said something was going to happen, in a huge percentage of cases, it wouldn't! I could stack the deck in my favor for the characteristics I was trying to draw out, but I was still never sure what I'd get in the whelping box.

That unpredictability is one of the things that keeps breeding interesting. Breeders are all trying to accomplish a goal, but at the same time it's not something that you can really do without outside intervention. I often pray about my breeding decisions, and I do feel like I'm led by God when I make good decisions about my dogs. There are times when getting my attention is the main problem, of course. I have a tendency to be thick-headed—I'm not quite as intelligent as the Kari line, I tend to take after the Ursa line. So sometimes He has to really knock hard! "Hey, Tina! Where are you going?" That's when I have to rethink my choices, and let Him lead the way.

Sometimes He leads me in ways I never would have imagined.

Foundation Dog Pictures

Kari and Boeg (Kari line)

Luke and Lisa (Ursa Line)

(Ria Line)

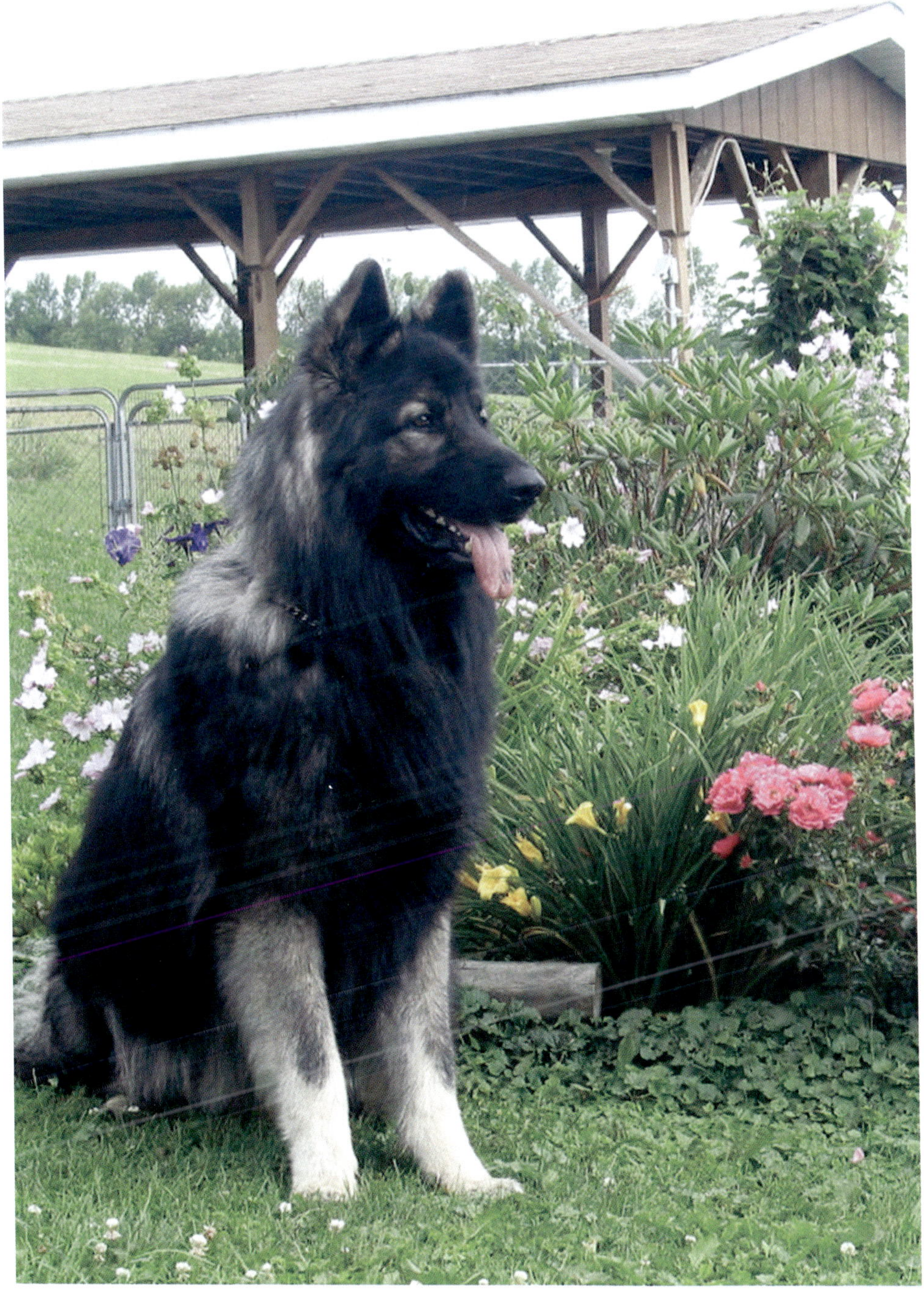

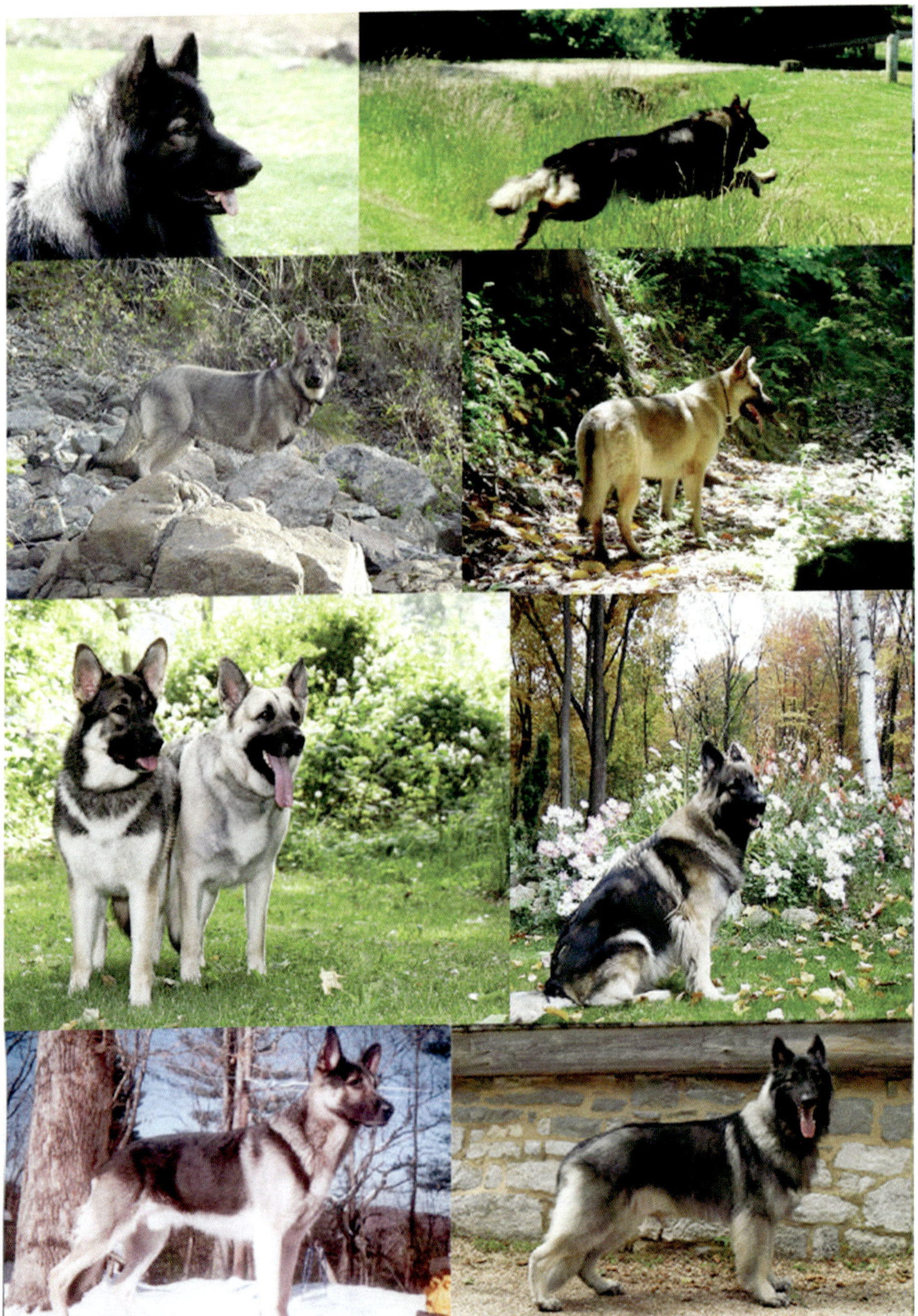

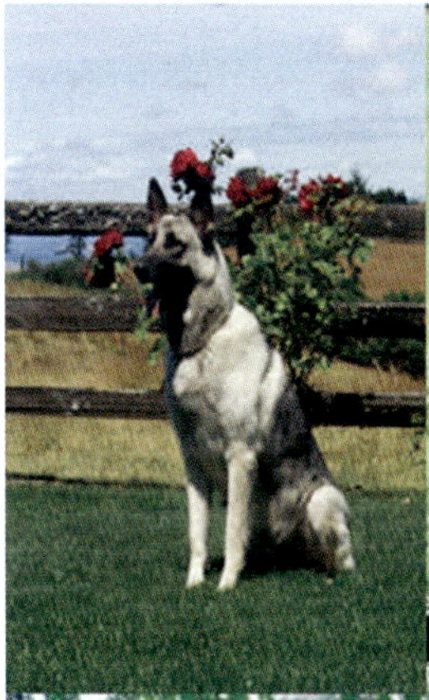
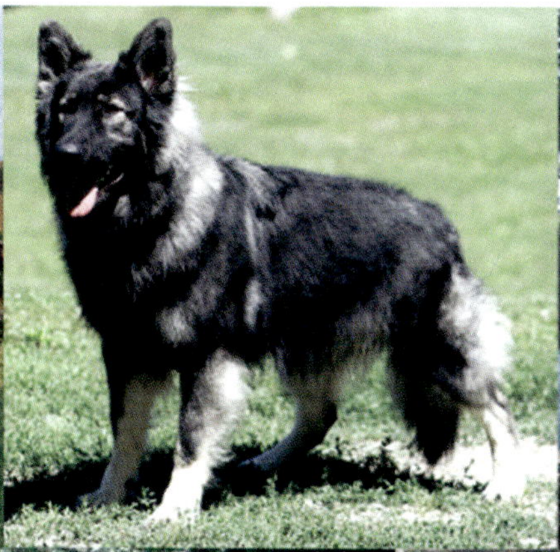
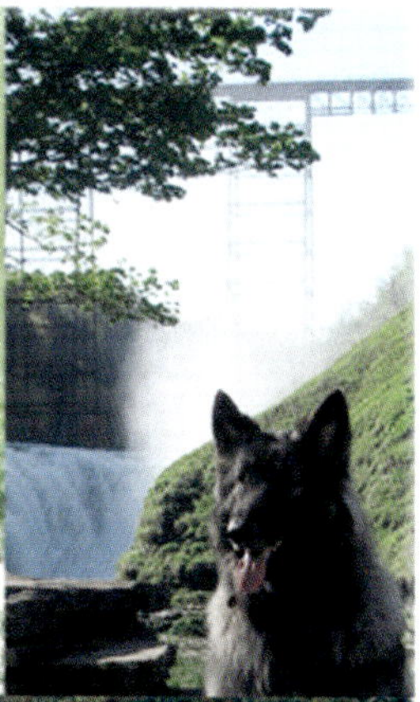
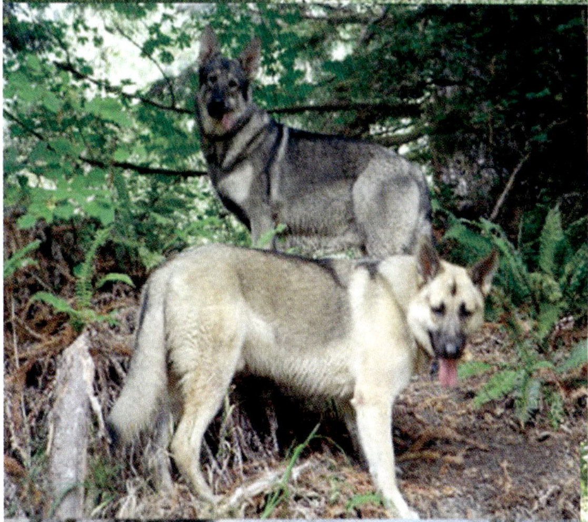
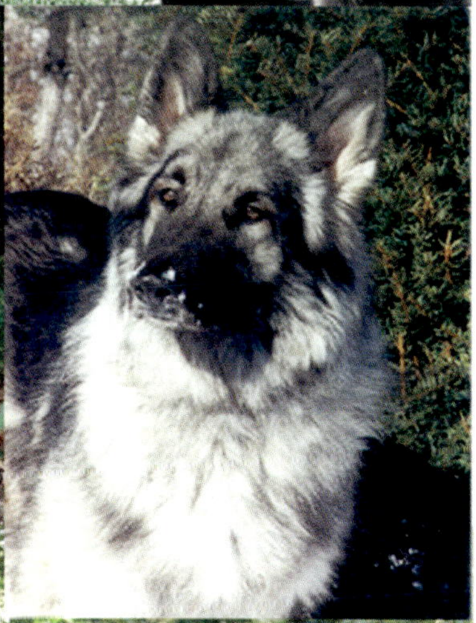
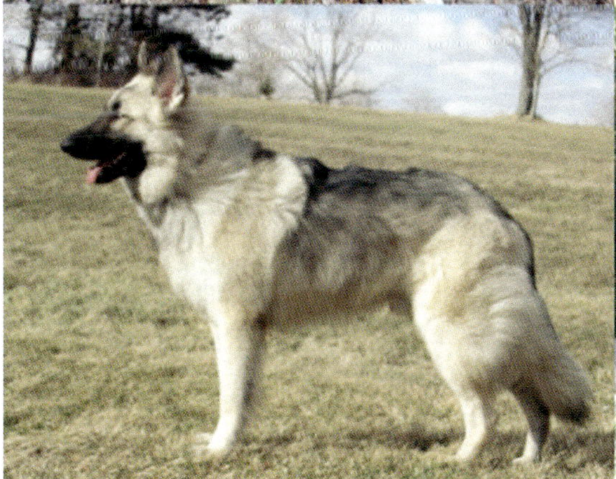
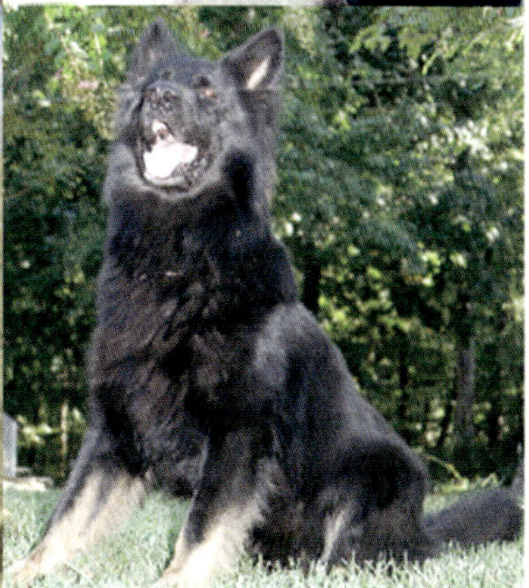

78 THE SHILOH SHEPHERD STORY

Letting Go of the AKC

By this time I'd had twenty-eight years of experience with the American Kennel Club. Not all of it was good experience. The AKC is taking steps to correct their problems now, but back in the '70s and '80s there was almost no control. You could purchase a puppy from a pet shop or a wholesaler who would provide you with "AKC papers" that might not even belong to the particular puppy you had purchased! The AKC was not adequately monitoring genetic defects in dogs, and they allowed anyone to receive full breeding rights on any dog they owned, regardless of genetic faults.

Don Baker's words still ring my ears: "Paper don't refuse ink!" What does that mean? Simply put, whatever you write on your litter forms, the AKC will accept as long as you include proper payment. There was absolutely no accountability.

The changes that I was seeing in the Shiloh Shepherd made me think that our days were numbered as AKC German Shepherds. That feeling got even stronger when I saw what was going on with my satellite breeders.

As the popularity of Shiloh Shepherds grew, many of my satellite breeders insisted on crossing Shilohs with their incompatible "regular" German Shepherd stock, thinking that if it was okay with the AKC, it was okay with me. But I had begun to see, even if my satellite breeders didn't, that regular AKC stock was just not good enough. If I allowed this breeding back to non-Shiloh German Shepherds to continue, at best the dogs would be "non-Shilohs," and I would not want them to carry the name. At worst, they would have the health and temperament problems that I had encountered when I had crossed Shilohs to GSDs myself in the '70s. If dogs like that were coming from my satellite breeders with the name "Shiloh Shepherd" attached to them, they would certainly shed a bad light on my kennel name, as well as the real Shilohs.

I had worked too hard to let that happen.

The AKC German Shepherd had too much genepool to be controllable—hundreds of thousands of dogs. The reason I had kept such detailed records for so many years was so we could know exactly what we were dealing with. The Shiloh Shepherd could not retain the qualities I was striving for if people kept adding in dogs without the huge amount of LMX data required for a Shiloh. I had to think of another plan.

Pondering a Split

Once I got the foundation lines down, and the Ria, Kari, and Ursa lines were working, I knew I was soon going to get to a point where my breeding would hit a brick wall. Since our gene pool was deliberately small, very soon it was going to be dangerous to breed my stock, because the dogs would be too closely related. Then recessive health problems could start popping up. It was time to look for new blood.

Back in the '70s, I had tried most of the American German Shepherd lines, as well as some of the more notable lines from Germany, with no success; in fact, time after time, those dogs were disappointing failures. I knew for sure that those lines were not what I wanted for my outcross.

Then one day a radical thought occurred to me: why not bring in another breed of dog altogether?

I knew that the Shiloh lines were strong enough that they could handle an influx of entirely new blood and still be Shilohs. The idea of bringing in another type of dog was extremely exciting—I could bring in a big dog, like a Malamute, and solidify the size I was looking for once and for all! I could take my giant German Shepherds, and add a little vein of something else, and create something new—a separate breed!

It was an exciting idea, but very scary too. Bringing in another breed of dog would mean cutting my ties with the AKC: as far as the AKC was concerned, my dogs would be mutts.

I spent almost two years thinking and praying about leaving the AKC and striking out on my own. I did a lot of background research. I knew that if I was going to break away I would have to set up my own database, but I didn't know anything about computers. That was a big problem. Managing an entire breed of dogs is extremely complicated. But in my mind I still felt like I was heading away from the AKC. I was looking for an open door.

Back in the late '80s anyone would have told you that leaving the AKC would be horrendously stupid and dangerous. I'd lose AKC papers, and then I'd have nothing. My dogs would not be papered anymore. Who's going to buy dogs without papers? If they don't have AKC papers, they're mongrels! And I was thinking about breeding in a Malamute mix too? I mean, think about it, logically!

Meanwhile, I had over a hundred dogs in my kennel. The overhead on my property was almost $180,000 a year, including dog food, medications, advertisements, kennel help, electric bills, long-distance phone bills, vet bills, transports, printing, and postage. That is what I had to pay out just to maintain where I was. I knew that if I left the AKC, I could bet on losing at least a third of my business right away.

You can see why I didn't tell many people about my idea.

I continued to think it over, and pray about it. I was looking for a sign. Was leaving the AKC really the right thing to do? I thought that the Shiloh Shepherd had enough of a reputation, and enough of a client base, that I could keep going without the AKC. The dogs wouldn't change. The name wouldn't change. The only thing that would change was the fact that they would be registered independently of the AKC.

I pondered the idea for quite a while as I went about my daily work. It was my secret, and it was never far from my mind.

Lisa and Samson in the training center.

Chapter 5

New Directions

Looking for an Outcross

Bringing in an outcross, a totally unrelated dog, works like a purification for the gene pool. In a way it's like a blood transfusion, which gets rid of various genes you may be compounding by inbreeding. After you do it, you inbreed back in quickly, and you should be able to get your dogs back to where you had them, only they'll be even stronger.

To find my outcross I researched the strongest American German Shepherd lines, to see if I could find any dogs that I really liked. In the '80s, Pacific Gold was one of the famous German Shepherd dogs I was thinking about bringing into the gene pool. I'd seen a lot of pictures of him in the *German Shepherd Review*, but never in person, so I went to see him at a show. As I approached him, the handler's assistant came up from behind the dog to bring a brush for him, and the dog jumped about six feet—he totally freaked because there was somebody coming up from behind him. I thought, Uh oh, temperament problems! And I just walked away.

During the early '80s I made other attempts at outcrossing back to the world's most famous German imports, as well as to the best American and Canadian champions, but I got very poor results every single time. One dog I outcrossed was Giant Killer. He carried a fantastic pedigree and had produced some huge solid blacks. I felt he would blend nicely with my UFO line. What I didn't know about Giant Killer was what he was carrying in his genes: Sub-aortic stenosis and bloat.

Bloat will hit a seemingly healthy dog harder than a heart attack, and cause excruciating pain, often resulting in death. When an owner finds his young healthy dog in severe pain, bloated, unable to move properly, trying to vomit nothing, it is horrifying. If a family pet bloats during the night, the owners will most likely find him stiff by morning.

Bloat is common among German Shepherds, and in theory it could happen to any dog. But like canine hip dysplasia, bloat also has genetic roots, and some lines are more prone to succumb to it than others. No breeder worth her salt would ever inbreed on a dog that is known to be carrying such a disease. And that's what Giant Killer brought with him.

Giant Killer turned out to be a very problematic dog. The sub-aortic stenosis and bloat problems that he brought into my gene pool plagued me for over a decade. Even today I am careful that none of my licensed breeders inbreed on dogs from the Giant Killer line. Giant Killer was the dog that finally set my mind against using famous German Shepherds for our outcross.

After so much rapid success with the Shiloh gene pool, most of my outcross attempts were very frustrating. I wasn't going forward, I was going backward. That experience is why I get so frustrated when people splinter off from my breeding program and start breeding Shilohs to traditional German Shepherds. I try to tell them, "It's not going to work! You're not going to make progress by beating your head into that wall!" Believe me, I tried just about everything.

I went on looking for an outcross, but success came only when I went in a totally different direction.

Samson and Sabrina

Peter, a friend of mine in the Yukon, had been experimenting with a well-known strain of Giant Malamutes. Those dogs had good hips, but they didn't possess the intelligence and willingness to work that he wanted. Since Peter had access to an old line of super-intelligent German Shepherd dogs, with one of the London ancestors in it (as Kari also did), he started crossing these lines with his Malamutes, and seemed very happy with the results. Peter also maintained detailed records of the LMX data within his lines. That really got me thinking.

Since I was nearly certain that a split from the AKC was in our future, I decided to take the plunge and give Peter's Malamute lines a try. Peter was also a Christian, so I felt that I could certainly trust him. He did a breeding for me with one of his dogs and produced Samson, whom we called "the MAW

London dogs

line." The MAW line gave me some very successful litters, and I felt encouraged.

Then, by accident, I discovered a line of dogs that Don Baker had developed, another line of old Wurttemberger-type German Shepherds that were heavy boned. Don had a thirty-year program of breeding his "Texas Woolies," which were definitely from the old lines. I knew for a fact there was Sarplaninac in Don's lines, which is a big, heavy dog that's got floppy ears, an old flock guardian dog that is still highly regarded by herdsman in Europe. I knew we were going to have some problems with the ears and the tails, and I wasn't happy with their temperaments, but I thought my lines could overcome those problems. Otherwise, to me Don's Texas Woolies looked good.

I spent many days with Don, researching his lines, discussing the dogs in his pedigree, looking at pictures of his dogs and of the puppies they produced, and of littermates as they matured. Don had a plan that he had been following for many decades, and he was generous in sharing his knowledge about his lines, including their faults and virtues, so that I would be able to utilize his gene pool to its best advantage. A good breeder is one who knows how to be honest, and Don is a good breeder.

I bred Sabrina, my choice from Don's lines, to my Smokey, and, aside from heavy ears, which I had expected, the dogs weren't bad. I thought Smoke would give me better temperament, but I thought the Kari line would give me better ears, so I allowed Sabrina to breed one more time. We bred to the Kari line, and that's where we got Captain. Then I took the Kari line, went back into the Smoke line with that gene pool, went forward with that, and that's what worked! It boned up what I already had, and it gave the progeny good legs, good strong ears, better temperament, and a better head. All the qualities the Texas Wooly line was missing, the Shiloh improved on, but the Shiloh line was missing more bone, and that's what the Texas Woolies gave me back.

Since I liked what I had gotten from the pure Sabrina/Smoke (Ursa line) and Sabrina/Shane (Kari line) crossings I had done, I bred Sabrina directly to Samson and I kept four pups from that litter to be used in my upcoming gene pool expansion program. Those puppies were Bria, Sheba, Snow and Goliath. Then I used those dogs to cross back into my Kari-Ursa-Ria lines to intensify the bone, height, hips and the intelligence that both Samson and Kari were strengthening in all of their descendants.

The outcross was done.

One of the things that all breeders learn early on in their careers is that when you outcross two inbred lines you get awesome results, as long as they are compatible. If they are not compatible, you get disasters. The only reason the Texas Wooly Sabrina line and the Malamute-based Samson line worked was because they both came from established, carefully-researched inbred lines, just like my dogs. Once you get a good combination, you know it for sure.

First Steps for a New Breed

Once I brought in Samson, I knew that I needed to make that jump away from the AKC. But how? I spent a lot of time thinking about all my records. All that gene pool, all those littermate x-rays, temperament, size, and recessives for each and every dog—data going all the way back to the '60s! I had no idea how to get all that into a computer program.

I talked to some computer programmers who were capable of designing a program to do the basic database job, but they were quoting me forty, fifty, sixty thousand dollars for the level of complexity that I would require. That was out of the question. I had an Apple IIE, where I kept address records of my clients, I remember it had a green screen—very low tech! I was not prepared to do the job myself. So I just prayed about it. I said, Lord, if you want me to make this break from the AKC, you're going to have to provide a way.

I waited for the Lord to intervene, but I didn't see an answer.

Eventually I found what seemed to be a good solution. At a dog show, I met a group called The Federation of International Canines, or FIC. They had a computer-based program and they said they could help me get my registry going, but they couldn't do my littermate x-ray records (LMX), because their computer system didn't have the capabilities. I would have to maintain my own records, and they would issue papers. That sounded good enough for the time being. So on September 1, 1990, the FIC agreed to register the "Shiloh Shepherd," named for its kennel of origin. After twenty-eight years, it seemed like we were finally on our way.

***

If you're going to have a breed, you need to promote it, and you have to have a group of people who are behind the breed. A dog club is for owners who want to show off their dogs at the shows; it's also responsible for educating new breeders, as well as future owners. In June 1991, I incorporated the Shiloh Shepherd Dog Club of America, Inc. (SSDCA). We had eighteen members who wanted to show and breed, located from New York to California. We gathered yearly at my house for Homecoming, and we met at all the shows. Membership increased steadily, month by month.

My fellow Shiloh Shepherd Dog Club of America members and I began by taking on the challenge of protecting the Shiloh Shepherd from backyard breeders. We introduced a strict breeders' code to protect the future generations: Shiloh Shepherd puppies could be sold only to signers of the breed code, or as pets on neuter/spay agreements. Each dog used for breeding after 1992 would have to be evaluated by the SSDCA "breed warden" (me) for temperament and conformation as well as genetic makeup before it could receive full breeding rights.

I also told the club right from the beginning that the club should give recognition to the real creator of the Shiloh Shepherd—Jehovah. The original membership fully embraced this concept and made sure that it was written into the constitution that the fish symbol would always be a part of our club logo. The club got off to a great start, and I thought things were looking good for the breed to make significant progress in the 1990s.

But something was already going wrong.

***

In 1991, less than a year after they took over our registry, it was clear that there was a problem at the Federation of International Canines. After several undeserving dogs had received breeding papers, I began investigating. I found that the FIC had been issuing certificates for dogs that were not eligible. They were even issuing papers for dogs that didn't have their hip data in yet! Basically, if a breeder paid them twenty dollars, the FIC would send out a piece of paper. And if the breeder told them the dog was a poodle, that's what they'd say it was.

That was not how I had intended our registry to work.

So I went on my riot act, like back in my biker days, and I told the owner of the FIC, "You do this and I'll break your neck." I took everything back. Certainly a registry should not consist of just a computer spitting out certificates; I could have done that on my Apple IIE. But that's what the FIC was.

I cancelled the agreement, took back the data from the FIC, and started the International Shiloh Shepherd Registry in July of 1991. All of the Shiloh Shepherd Dog Club of America members signed an agreement of allegiance to the ISSR. I didn't love the idea of running my own registry—I was already much too busy. But now I knew that I couldn't trust my data to just anyone. I would do it myself until the Lord provided a better way.

Once the ISSR was in place, there was only one thing left to do.

The Final AKC Breakaway

In 1993 I made a controversial announcement to the SSDCA membership: "Nobody's going to get AKC papers anymore, and all the AKC papers need to be turned in. If you've still got AKC papers on your dog, you've got to turn them in if you want ISSR papers. If you don't, you're not going to get ISSR papers, ever."

It was a big shakedown. What I was requesting was a bit like a mass citizenship change, and the idea didn't go over well with some of my satellite breeders. Many were afraid to venture into new territory, and preferred to stay with the AKC. It was a stressful time to see how many good people would still stay with the program. I watched a few good dogs get lost from the gene pool, which was depressing. We did indeed lose some momentum in 1993.

A lot of people didn't want to admit that they didn't want to give up their AKC papers, so they just went into hiding. I guess they were thinking, "I don't want Tina to know that I didn't do it, because she might ask me, and I don't want to lie to her, and I don't want to give up my AKC papers. So I'll just hide for a while."

I lost some friends when I left the AKC.

Many of my German Shepherd friends felt that I had betrayed them by splitting off. Instead of trying to fix the problems with the German Shepherd dog, I had just gone out and done my own thing. Some of them would bad-mouth the Shilohs, saying "Oh, they're nothing—they're just an oversized, clumsy dog, they don't have the drive, the spirit. They're just reject German Shepherds that should not have any kind of papers."

I took that in stride, because that's competition. It's like saying Fords are better than Chevrolets; you expect that kind of thing.

But the people who stuck with the program were excited. The dedicated few were on fire with great hopes for the future! We were starting our own breed, and we were going to go forward no matter what. I told people that it was sort of like crossing from Boston to California in the pioneer times. Some of those dogs would live on forever as part of the foundation that developed this breed.

Splitting from the AKC was not easy, for me or for anybody. It was scary. But the breeders who dared to make that jump in 1993, and the others that joined them later and remained true to the vision, are the people we all can thank for the Shilohs of today.

Sharing My Testimony

We continued to hit the shows and expos, and more and more people were drawn to the Shilohs, like moths to a burning light at night. Those of us who were producing puppies could never keep up with the demand. It seemed like everyone who met a Shiloh in person wanted one.

Our club continued to grow, and I spent all of my time traveling. I flew all over the country—Atlanta, Orlando, Dallas, Seattle, L.A.—going to just about

Back cover of a Shiloh Shepherd Dog Club of America, Inc. Newsletter from the mid '90s.

90 THE SHILOH SHEPHERD STORY

Early shows: 1990-91 as published in the SSDCA newsletter.

1993: Tina Barber wins first ARBA Breeder of the Year Award.

every dog show to promote the breed. It almost bankrupted me. I was getting expos going, getting shows going, I explained our breed standard at judge seminars, I tried to get more people that owned Shilohs to come to the shows. I went to pet expos, put up booths, handed out literature. It was extremely hectic and busy.

Then one day I got a call from a lady who was getting one of my pups. She called about her puppy, and we ended up talking for three hours about the Lord. At the end of our conversation she said that I had really helped her spiritually, and that she felt my answers were a Godsend.

I realized then that my original deal with the Lord was, You give me the miracle, and I will glorify Your name... and I wasn't doing my part. I realized that I had to devote more time to helping people through God's word. That was the beginning of my phone counseling sessions, which have continued to this day.

I let people know that I was available if they just needed somebody to talk to, even at two o'clock in the morning. People would call me and say, "Well, I don't want to talk to you about dogs, I've got some Bible questions to ask you." And I'd drop whatever I was doing, I didn't care what it was, and if the phone was bleeping because people were calling to buy puppies I ignored them, because the Lord had to remain my Number One priority.

I was glad to have a spiritual connection with some of my clients as things got crazier for me. I had no idea at the time how much I would come to lean on those people.

Lisa with four dogs, on the road.

Political Woes Begin

Our club, the SSDCA, was growing like crazy, drawing members from coast to coast. Some were breeders, and the others were people that wanted to help out and participate. I was running the organization and providing the funds.

Then one day the club secretary's roof started leaking, and she needed money to fix it. So she took the money that I had put into the SSDCA account for the club's bills, and paid for her emergency home improvement. I discovered that when I found that the funds that I had put in towards the bills were gone—and so was the secretary.

People had been worried for a while about me being in charge of the club. Because I was the breed warden, they thought that maybe I shouldn't be too politically powerful. After the fiasco with the secretary, I started to listen to suggestions that maybe I should step aside as club leader.

I should have seen what was coming next.

The man who was my vice president at the time offered to help out with the club, so I turned all of the paperwork over to him. He then collected all of the renewals and sold "works" packages, consisting of my little book and color picture collage. I continued to pay for all the printing, ads, and so on. They moved the club headquarters down to Kentucky from upstate New York.

Then when I drove to Kentucky in June 1992 for an accounting, I found that my vice president was trying to have me removed as president so that he could take over the club! I was shocked, though I could see later that I shouldn't have been.

I have pretty strict breeding rules about how often dogs can be bred, and who breeds to whom. It would certainly have been possible to make a lot more money without those rules. The demand for Shilohs was staggeringly high, so people's greed was starting to get the best of them; this was the beginning of a pattern that I would continue to see for the next thirteen years.

But of course, money was not, and is not, the point of the Shiloh Shepherd.

The fight went on over the next seven months. We were forced to go to court to get rid of that vice president. I spent a lot of money on legal fees, phone bills, printing... We ended up having to change the constitution in order to get my vice president and his self-appointed new board of directors out, and all the SSDCA members had to re-vote. People came to New York from as far away as Wisconsin for the vote, and those who couldn't show up FedExed in their voting ballots. The vote was unanimous in my favor. My former vice president ended up keeping the money from the club, but the Postmaster General closed the Kentucky P.O. box. The club moved forward again.

That was my first real experience dealing with "club politics," and it certainly was not something that I ever wanted to contend with again. After that long battle, a lot of people got discouraged with the club. They said things like, "Oh boy, now you've got a club going, but you've got all these political hassles. Do we really want to deal with this?" It caused some people to not even become involved, and other people to walk away. I lost several long-time Shiloh breeders and their gene pools to this foolish controversy, which was much more upsetting than my own loss of money and time.

I was feeling discouraged. But it was around that time that another of my prayers was unexpectedly answered.

Enter the TCCP

One day I was talking to one of my long-time clients, Stephen Betcher, about my situation, and I was moaning about how hard it was for me to run a registry out of my home on top of all my other responsibilities. And he said, "Well, you know, my wife Barbara is a professional programmer, why don't I ask her if she can help?"

It turned out that the two of them owned a company in Texas called The Complete Computer Place (TCCP). Barbara called me, and I told her what I wanted the computer to do, including complete data management

Stephen Betcher and Mona's Lisa of Better-Ways at Homecoming

for the LMX program and all of its components. I said, "This is my miracle plan, my fantasy program. Can you design this thing for me?"

She said that we could give it a shot.

It ended up taking us almost a year to put the program together, because there were a million little decisions that needed to be made. For example, dogs could have only three letters for their papers, so they ended up with ORA for orange, gold dogs got GOL, pink papered got PIN; we had a coding system for co-ownerships, breeders' agreements... There was an incredible amount of detail work to do.

Barbara also designed the system to track dominant and recessive faults and virtues, in order to allow future breeders to get a good glimpse of the shadow dog in their pedigrees. This program was called LMI (Litter Mate Information), and it was an expansion of the original LMX program. It was, and is, a wonderful resource.

Stephen Betcher was a retired Army supply sergeant, and military precision was his style. He offered to put all of the data into our new database, so all of my thousands of files went to Texas. Stephen spent hours and hours every day punching in data. By the end of the decade we had fully documented data on thousands of Shiloh Shepherds, as well as the names of thousands of ancestors! Every ISSR registration document lists detailed information about that dog's height, weight, color, coat, temperament, hip results, and more. This data is also recorded for each parent, grandparent, and other ancestors, and is reported in extended pedigrees.

Stephen was a sergeant all the way. He used to call my daughter up when she submitted paperwork wrong and say, "Get up against the wall! Assume the position!" He and I saw eye to eye: when it comes to data, everything has to be perfect.

After Stephen had done a huge number of listings, he would run off "alpha listings," or first drafts of the data (also known as Stud Book Reports), so that I could proofread them. I remember feeding my grandson Joshua when he was a baby, holding the bottle, and going piece by piece over the alpha listings for hours and hours, checking and double-checking any errors, looking for anything that might be missing. If Stephen had run into a brick wall—for example, if we had pedigree data to the eighth or ninth generation and it came to a dead end—I would fill in that data from my records, or I would research it in the old *German Shepherd Quarterlies*. I tracked down volumes of LMX data from my old breeders' books, pedigrees and memory. This went on for years.

Every couple of years I would get an alpha listing to go through, and

"Dream Computer" (excerpt from "Hip Dsyplasia: Them Bones Them Bones Them Hip Bones," published in winter 1983-84 *German Shepherd Quarterly* and reprinted in the 1986 *Shiloh Shepherd (Kennel) Stockbook*.

I realize this may sound crazy, but let's take a moment for a fantasy. What if an organization was formed by a group of dedicated breeders that proceded to compile (or program together) all the research done by all the various groups and organizations, then helped this foundation with their research by compiling all their knowledge and experience. For example, the results of breeding bitch A to stud 1 and the same bitch to stud 4, etc., encouraging all the big and small breeders to participate with added information. Everybody would submit all they know honestly (this is no time to advertise) for the benefit of improving the breed! Now the research center or foundation could enter all this data (tons and tons I hope) into the most complex computer available. Let's see what we've got here! Since this is MY fantasy, it would not be limited to hip dysplasia, but would include everything! A breeder could then call into the center and get data on hips, temperament, size, color, conformation, faults, virtues, etc., along with a full computer "fact sheet" recommending do's and don'ts for each dog they had. Actually, GSDCA has a somewhat similar program for their top-producing dogs. ...

My fantasy computer would contain similar information, but would include and emphasize specific data such as stud's name, number of bitches bred, number of puppies produced per litter, number of puppies x-rayed, actual results (OFA ratings), and percentages.

1986 Update: *Even though my "fantasy computer" never became a reality, the "LMX" program has gotten stronger and stronger. We are now breeding 6th and 7th generation LMX dogs! The program does a lot more than just give details about hips — it gives us a much better picture of the temperament, color, size, faults, and virtues we will be getting in each litter. This stock sheet includes our code, and several sample pedigrees for you to study, that explain how our program works for the benefit of the German Shepherd breed. Even though we still have not completely conquered the problem of hip dysplasia, we are now able to restrict it to a very small percentage of our lines, and we continually strive to completely eliminate it!! The main goal of this kennel has always been to produce the ultimate in intelligence and size... with sound hips!*

Note: *Mrs. Barbara Betcher, the owner of the TCCP, has not only developed Tina's dream program but has compiled all of her thirty-plus years of data into it, and, since 1993 has continued to maintain and expand the ISSR's database with strict military precision.*

Stephen Betcher was a man of many talents—he was sometimes referred to as a Renaissance Man. He joined the United States Army as a young man and served over twenty years. He served his country with pride. He was in Vietnam during the war, stationed in Korea three tours and Germany one tour.

When Stephen retired from the Army he wanted to raise dogs. His first adventure was raising white German Shepherds. This is how he first learned about Tina Barber. She had an ad in *Dog World* showing white Shiloh Shepherds would be available. Stephen and Tina talked for many months and they became fast friends. Stephen was a true advocate for the Shiloh Shepherd breed and Tina Barber.

His first Shiloh was a female, Morris Good Morning Mona, who was with pups when he got her. She had several female pups, one of which, Lady, is still with me. His next Shiloh was GV NS abiCH Zion's Endeavor Of Better Ways (Fred) who is also still with me. Stephen bred a good number of pups, and he treated each one as his own.

He was steadfast, determined, stubborn, sometimes harsh, but kind and loving to those he knew. Many Shiloh owners saw these same characteristics when Stephen was working on paperwork or trying to solve a registration problem. He wanted information to be correct and handled properly and would make every effort to see that this happened.

—by Barbara Betcher

that's the way we worked, back and forth. Eventually we got all of the ancestral GSD records and ISSR Shiloh Shepherds registered. Taken together, we presently have over 45,000 names in the ISSR's genetic database.

The complex program that Barbara designed would have cost me many thousands of dollars. From the start the ISSR and TCCP have had a contract in place, and funds derived from registrations are used to pay for the professional data processing services provided by TCCP.

As for Stephen, he saved every tiny piece of paper relating to the Shiloh Shepherds and he kept all the files documented and accounted for. If something had to be changed, I would have to send him a memorandum for record (MFR), and he attached the MFR to the record to say why he made that change. It was always done with strict military precision.

Stephen Betcher was one of the most dedicated people I have ever had the pleasure to know. He spent over a decade of his life protecting the future welfare of his beloved dogs. Stephen and Barbara worked together and each knew the other's responsibilities; this has enabled Barbara to keep up the work Stephen started. It is because of the honest integrity of people like Stephen and Barbara Betcher that I have been able to continue in this business in spite of all its problems. The TCCP processes the ISSR data with military precision. I couldn't ask for anything better in this world.

In other areas of my life, however, I was not having as much success.

Very Important Breeders

I had my outcrosses, but I knew it would take three generations in order to properly expand my gene pool. Once I started using Samson and Sabrina, I focused on expansion.

In order to expand the gene pool, I needed to have numbers. I had to have variety. At the time of the AKC split I had over a hundred dogs in my own kennel, and I probably could have produced thirty-five or forty litters a year if I had really pushed it to the limits. But I knew that even that wouldn't be enough. I would need about seventy litters a year, for ten years, in order to establish a decent gene pool base.

For that, I would need some help.

I didn't think it would be too hard: I figured that if I could get twenty-five or thirty breeders, and they each had two litters a year under a controlled environment, I could easily meet my goals. I could cut back on my own

Laz.

breeding, and just monitor what the other people were doing. We could get the job done together, and have enough base out there to look forward to becoming a real breed.

In the beginning, it wasn't hard at all. Since the Shiloh Shepherd puppies had already been selling for thousands of dollars, it was not difficult to find people who felt inclined to try breeding. But I felt that these people needed a strong education, so I started the "Very Important Breeders" program.

I began it with my former satellite breeders who had stuck around after the AKC switch. In order to give them a little more responsibility than just whelping puppies for me, I gave them each a bitch to own. They would have the puppies, and I would give them the clients to sell the puppies to. They would set the prices, as per the SSDCA guidelines, and make the sale. All I asked was that they follow up with their clients in order to find out how the dogs' hips were doing and if there were any genetic problems. I provided them with an opportunity to make thousands of dollars on each puppy they sold. All they had to do was maintain proper documented data.

They liked the deal. Right away, instead of getting four hundred dollars a puppy, some of them started getting three thousand dollars a puppy.

My original school for the VIB program was a bit crude. I made copies of booklets like *Planned Breeding*, by Lloyd Brackett, and typed out pages of lessons and pedigrees that I would mail out to my group of licensed breeders, in order to help them get more familiar with our program. I included tests that they had to complete and return for scoring. I was trying to teach them everything I had ever learned, including genetics, so that even beginners could avoid some of the horrible pitfalls normally associated with dog breeding. I never charged a penny for my time and knowledge—not even for the postage and printing cost I incurred with each set of lessons.

Well, this was a learning experience for me. I learned that there were a few good breeders, but for a lot of them, it just wasn't in their hearts. What was in their hearts was money! I knew by now that if their hearts were not in the right place, there was no way I could trust them to make the right decisions for the future of the breed. In fact, many of those people shouldn't have been breeding at all.

The problem was, once they started making all that money, they were more determined than ever to breed Shiloh Shepherds.

Breeders Lose Control

Shilohs were skyrocketing in popularity. For a while there were ten clients for every puppy born. People were buying puppies for thirty-five hundred dollars each, and nobody was blinking an eye. The breeders started overpricing the puppies. I told them, "Whoa, you guys are going way out on a limb. You're selling pet-quality puppies for top show-quality prices. You're ripping off the public."

They didn't want to hear it. They said, "The public wants to pay our price, let them pay it." I was not happy with that, but the momentum was there, and everybody wanted a Shiloh. Because breeders were looking at it like—wait a minute, ten puppies a litter, at thirty-five hundred dollars a puppy, that's thirty-five thousand bucks a litter! If I have three litters a year, holy cow! Wouldn't you like to make that kind of money, a hundred thousand dollars a year, to sit home, watch television, just have a few puppies around? Doesn't that sound cool?

Most breeders of purebreds got an average of four hundred dollars a puppy. Breeders selling ISSR Shiloh Shepherd puppies were averaging fifteen hundred to three thousand dollars a puppy—sometimes more. That was because the dogs had the Shiloh Shepherd name, the Shiloh Shepherd advertising, and most importantly, Shiloh Shepherd breeding and detailed pedigrees. All my breeders had to do was collect their money and follow the rules.

> New "rare breed" clubs and "registries" seem to be popping up faster than weeds on most country lawns. Anyone can find an unspayed female dog, then breed her to a friend's dog that resembles some unknown/rare breed and then sell those pups for thousands of dollars. Self-proclaimed "registries" are willing to issue a paper to anyone willing to pay for it, and they don't care about maintaining proper genetic documentation on any particular breed. Most require only a handwritten pedigree and a check or money order to register the dog. And anyone can claim to be a "registry" and print off papers on their home PC, as there are no laws to prevent them. All they have to do is pick out a popular "rare breed" name and set up shop.
>
> If you don't take the time to investigate, you could be duped into paying thousands of dollars for a mixed breed puppy. Never accept anything you read on the Internet at face value. Ask for data that can honestly validate the entire breed's history over several decades.
>
> The ISSR was the original breed registry formed in 1991. Since then there have been other self-proclaimed Shiloh Shepherd registries that have come and gone. It is important to note that since the Shiloh Shepherd breed is still under development, and because there is very little information regarding these other registries, the importance of learning about the breed and the breeder before you buy cannot be stressed enough.

It did not take me long to figure out that many of my breeders were selling their pet quality pups with gold papers—gold papers mean a dog can be bred, and gold-papered dogs are worth more money. Once I started investigating what was going on, and tried to work with these breeders to help them to evaluate their pups properly, I realized that I was being tagged as the super bitch of the century! I got the feeling that some of my breeders wanted me out of the picture.

I had opened up and shared a lot of secrets with my Very Important Breeders, giving them access to my genetic information—my "secret recipe," so to speak. Slowly, it dawned on me that if I couldn't trust my own breeders, I was going to be in a world of trouble, because I had no control over what people could do in the name of Shiloh Shepherds. In life, there are laws against trademark infringement. But in dog breeding, there are no laws. If someone steals your name in dog breeding, you can call him or her a thief in public if it

Cherry Blossom Classic.

makes you feel better, but the law won't protect you.

I felt a storm brewing.

Cherry Blossom Classic

When the public had a chance to meet the dogs, people were so impressed they often asked for pups on the spot. The dogs just kept getting more popular. Prices for show puppies rose dramatically, because people just kept buying them. Breeders were gearing up for mass production. Nineteen ninety-five was a great year for the Shiloh Shepherd.

When I went to the Cherry Blossom Classic that year in 1995, we had fifty-six Shiloh Shepherd entries, a pretty good number for a rare breed show. I remember watching the whole ring full of dogs in the final class for best of breed competition. They were impressive looking, very beautiful. The crème de la crème of the Shiloh world at that time was there: dogs like Captain, Warrior, and Orso.

What I didn't know was, that was the last time I'd have that feeling for quite a while.

Tension Increases

I needed other people to be involved with breeding Shilohs, so that there would be enough dogs out there for anyone who wanted to own one, and also so that we could quickly solidify our gene pool. But even though I knew I needed other breeders, I was finding it really difficult to work with some of them.

People have a phobia about being controlled, which is understandable.

However, I have always been straightforward as a leader. I told my breeders, "Here are the rules. You must follow them. Breeders who want to do their own thing are welcome to; they just can't use the Shiloh Shepherd name." I thought that was more than fair.

But I kept encountering resistance, surprisingly often.

Breeding choices were one area of controversy between me and my co-breeders. It was critical to my program that I keep all breeding matches under tight control. When the Shiloh Shepherd breed is finished, that might be a different matter, but while it's under development, somebody's got to be in charge of the way things are going. This often meant that I had to tell my breeders not to do something they wanted to do: "No, your bitch is not going to be compatible with that dog, I don't care if you think he's cute, or if your bitch is madly in love with him. Genetically, they're not compatible."

People didn't want to hear it. They'd say things like, "But she loves him. She doesn't want to breed to Yodo over there. We don't like him. He's too dark."

I had, and still have, some good, respectful breeders. But I've had some weird ones too. The foolish ones didn't want to look at the genetics, and they didn't want to consider the fact that I was looking at the long-term quality of the breed. I got a lot of "Who does Tina think she is?"

I'm somebody who knows better. I've been through the storms. It's just that simple.

It's like your mother says, "Honey, this is Prince Henry's son, he's worth a hundred million dollars. That guy over there has got a warrant out for his arrest for being a child molester. I would like you to date this man, not that one." Your mother's looking at it from a whole different perspective, which is, that man's going to give you a wonderful lifestyle, he's going to give you all the financial advantages you'd ever want, whereas, this guy's going to be in jail, and you're going to be on the street. But you're thinking, but he's cute! And he's got a sexy bike! I think that's the mentality that many novice breeders apply to dog breeding.

Then to my great surprise, my next club vice president after the Kentucky fiasco tried to pull off a coup d'etat at one of our Homecomings. She stood up and made a speech about how they didn't want me to be a dictator any more, and they could do better. My mouth just fell open. This was happening at my Homecoming—I was the hostess!

This audacious woman had five or six people stand up with her. I guess they thought they were going to get the rest of the group to rally with them. I looked at them standing there, and basically, to be blunt, I was ready to revert to some of my "old" methods of problem solving, right in front of everybody.

I stood up and I told her, "Take your stuff, pack it up, and get out of this place, or I'll take you out—personally!" Then I said, "Anybody else want to stand? You can walk out that door with them." Nobody else left. She and her little band of dissidents stormed out in a huff, while the rest of the membership gave me a loud standing ovation. That was a great day!

But as the value of these magnificent dogs spiraled upward, people continued to be motivated by greed. I did not know it then, but even more difficult battles waited just around the corner.

Chapter 6

Breeding Amid Dissent

Back in Court

The biggest problem that most dog clubs have is disagreements among their leaders. This almost always ends with splinter groups breaking off. Throughout my career I had witnessed this phenomenon practically destroy many breeds. In 1996, it happened to me: three dissident Shiloh breeders started the "United Shiloh Shepherd Dog Club" and began outcrossing Shilohs to German Shepherd dogs, but selling them as Shiloh Shepherds.

I was infuriated.

We weren't with the AKC anymore, so technically the name was unprotected. But for over twenty years "Shiloh Shepherd" had meant something—and it didn't mean randomly-outcrossed dogs! Those rogue breeders started advertising as "Shiloh Shepherds" in *Dog World*. They even tried to have a specialty show.

We took them to court. One of our Shiloh Shepherd club members hired a lawyer in Pennsylvania, and the court upheld my common law rights to the words "Shiloh Shepherd." The court ordered the dissidents to find a new name to describe their dogs. After the court case ended, I wrote a letter to our membership, urging them to put the nastiness of the court battle behind them. I told them that I was adamant about keeping this club operating as one. As long as there was any breath left in me, I would not advocate a split of any kind.

Shortly thereafter the small former-Shiloh splinter group started calling their dogs "King Shepherds," and the American Rare Breed Association (ARBA) opened up many venues for them to be shown as a "new" rare breed!

I was extremely frustrated, but there was nothing I could do about that. I had to just grit my teeth and move on.

Time and Money

I was running on a very tight budget in those days. I was producing fewer puppies because I had to spend so much time on the road, but my overhead to maintain my property was still as high as ever. Financially, I was going through rough times.

I knew I should stop spending, but I kept on: it was crucial to me that we get over the hump, to the point where the dogs were nationally recognized. At the time I considered all of the show and promo expenses as my responsibility—after all, this was my breed, so I was responsible for seeing to it that the breed got the recognition that it deserved. But I was running out of money.

By this time the Shiloh Shepherd had been in the public eye continuously for over twenty years, from 1974 to 1996, and that cost money! I spent about fifty thousand dollars a year on promotion: events, shows, literature, demonstrations, and advertising. That's five hundred thousand dollars in ten years. If I spent five hundred thousand in ten years, how much have I spent in my nearly thirty years with the Shiloh Shepherd?

One and a half million! That is why starting a breed is not for the faint at heart.

Sometimes I'd torture myself by thinking, If I had taken that money and put it into the stock market, I'd be retired by now very comfortably and very rich, I wouldn't have to be getting another mortgage on my house. But the bottom line is, Why do people buy a Rolex? Because of the reputation the name has. My energy for all those years had gone into developing dogs that were worthy of an outstanding reputation; now I was spending every dime I had to make sure that people knew about those dogs.

When I asked my breeders if they could chip in for some of the club expenses, they requested an audit of club funds to confirm that my contributions were not out of proportion to theirs. Landers and Walczak CPA documented that from 1991 to 1996 the club had a total income of $52,584.16, and of this $36,244.99 was paid by me; that figure did not count shows, expos and other events that I attended to promote the breed. In 1996 the club had nearly 300 members, and I paid 70% of the expenses. The club membership fees

Eric Curlee, a freelance author and Shiloh enthusiast, wrote an article, "Run with the Big Dogs," about Shiloh Shepherds that appeared in the magazine *American Survival Guide*, Vol. 19 Issue 5, May 1997.

...This is where the "formidable dog" factor comes into play. Standing 30 to 32 inches at the shoulder, weighing in at 120 to 140+ pounds of solid muscle, with a beautiful black or dark brown sable coat that gives a wolf-like appearance, this dog says "LLLLEEEET'S GET READY TO RUMBLE!" just by showing up. The bad guys will walk away clean, believe me! The axiom "a good big man will beat a good little man every time" applies to dogs as well, and the bad boys know it. No one wants to fool with what looks like a wolf-dog on steroids. And yet, to their family "pack," they are totally stable and trustworthy, possessed with a loving, gentle nature. Tina comments:

"Future Shilohs will be trained as bodyguard dogs, for a very selective group of people that insist on only the very best! As time progresses you will find their popularity as a mentally sound protector will reach from coast to coast and eventually across the continents. These dogs possess such depth in their personalities that you have to do a lot of studying in order to understand all of their capabilities better."

Super Dog- Tina continues: "Aside from the fact that these dogs happen to be the best possible companion you could ever provide for your family, they are also one of the most versatile breeds you could ask for. With the superior intelligence they possess, along with their fantastic sense of smell, these dogs are highly acclaimed as the most capable search and rescue dogs you could ever ask for! To them, this type of work comes naturally, and even though they are very obedient as a rule, they seem to know just when to follow their own instincts. Working with such a dog is pure pleasure." And, "despite the foolish notion that large breeds are 'clumsy,' you will find the real Shilohs unbelievably agile!"

Ms. Barber notes that to understand the nature of these animals, one must know that the roots of the true German Shepherd go all the way back to the wolf. Though not a true wolf-dog in the sense of a modern wolf-dog hybrid (which are beautiful and intelligent but potentially dangerous), nevertheless original records show that the mongrel was crossed with the wolf hybrid to establish the foundation for the German Shepherd breed. It is only when we know this that we will be able to more fully understand the type of intelligence they possess.

didn't even cover the cost of printing and mailing the fancy newsletters that were sent out three times per year—never mind the magazine ads and other expenses.

The fact that we were no longer AKC-registered had some potential future owners slightly concerned, so it was imperative that our advertising and expos continue to educate the public. I was not just concerned with my own puppy sales, but with making sure that all of the other ISSR breeders found the right homes for the hundreds of puppies that they were producing. Most people were not using the Internet in those days, so all of the promo campaigns had to be planned the old-fashioned way, with literature and advertising blitzes.

I sat down and told my fellow breeders, "You guys are collecting unbelievable amounts of money for these puppies, but you haven't contributed towards the advertising. If I go broke, I'm going to stop promoting, and you're going to stop selling your puppies." I then suggested that they start paying a 5% commission on each puppy sold, so that the funds could be put into a co-op style advertising budget. It would only cost them between seventy-five and one hundred fifty dollars for each puppy sold, and it would take a large burden from off my shoulders.

It didn't work.

Pax at the Cherry Blossom Classic

A small group of breeders refused to join the Very Important Breeder program, because they didn't want to contribute at all. This caused some of the VIB's to start complaining about the rules. Meanwhile the non-VIB's complained that it wasn't fair that they weren't getting my referrals!

So I mortgaged my house to raise money, and I maxed out all my credit cards to raise more money. I borrowed everything I could borrow, trying to make it until the breed was established, so that I could spend more time back at home raising puppies. I cut expenses wherever I could, including canceling the insurance on my home. I always trusted the Lord to provide. If I needed something, I prayed my way through it. If it was meant to be, I got it, and if it wasn't, I didn't. But things were getting scary.

And then, from out of nowhere, disaster struck once more.

Genetic Defect?

Lazarus was a great dog. He came from the first litter of Captain and Lizzy, two other amazing dogs. Lazarus was the last dog that I showed myself. He was so push-button trained that all I had to do was touch him, and he would freeze in that position. "One step, one step, head up, head up!" When I got him to where I wanted him, I would just touch him, and he'd freeze like a statue. Lazarus is still the poster dog on the Shiloh Shepherd website.

Then there was a second breeding of Lazarus's parents, Captain and Lizzie, and Jimmy, one of the puppies, came down with sudden paralysis of his rear quarters and was put to sleep. Then Jimmy's brother Titan and sister Annie were taken to their vets with similar symptoms—sudden onset of paralysis, or ataxia in the hind end. They were falling down, couldn't make it up hills, couldn't make it down hills, only walked very slowly on even levels.

They ran x-rays at Tufts and discovered an anomaly in the puppies that the vets had never seen before. Annie had compression of the spinal cord, just like Jimmy. She was put down and her body donated to Cornell, where the surgeon, neurologist and pathologist performed a necropsy on her, which included decalcifying her vertebrae. The vets thought it might be a genetic defect, but they weren't sure.

The lady who had whelped the litter was spending lots of money trying to figure it out. Her husband was having a fit, the clients were screaming bloody murder, they wanted her to pay the vet bills, they wanted her to give them refunds... All hell broke loose, very quickly.

And then rumors started that there was a genetic defect running through the Shiloh Shepherd! This so-called "back issue" struck fear into people's hearts.

I confronted the rumors head-on. I told my breeders that we would unite in taking aggressive action by researching and eliminating potential traps from our gene pool. I spoke with Titan's vet, Dr. McDonnell, who advised me that the problems of these six dogs had a familial tendency, which seemed to indicate genetic involvement. The cartilage in their backs did not fit together properly. It had been seen in thoroughbred horses, but never in dogs before. In other words, the vets had no idea.

Captain (the sire of the fatal litter) was given a temporary breed warning: he could not appear in a pedigree for at least five generations for a planned breeding, thus protecting against the infiltration of a possible lethal gene. I began to monitor all of the Captain lines closely. At the time of the crisis we had a total of fifty-four Captain grandkids, with two more litters due. I knew that if none of those approximately seventy pups showed any signs of problems, we would be able to breathe a lot easier.

G.V. Ch Shiloh's Captain-Caliber Baker ROM

I was extremely cautious, but the whole time I suspected that the back problem was not a genetic mutation.

Genetically speaking, even if you're pulling a gene from way back in the line, the probability of an entire litter inheriting a lethal recessive gene is astronomically remote. Take, for example, the litter of mine that unexpectedly contained two black puppies. That litter had seven puppies, and two were solid black. Not every puppy in the litter was born solid black; that wouldn't happen. If the parents, grandparents, and great-grandparents were not black, there's no way a whole litter would come out that way, even if you were inbreeding. Likewise, even if you are inbreeding heavily, it would be extremely rare to see more than a small percentage of puppies inherit the same polygenic disease, especially if it has never appeared in the ancestral gene pool via any of the other related inbred litters. Genetic principles follow predetermined patterns.

So I searched for another cause.

I suspected the pond at the home of Lizzie's owners. The litter was born in the summer, and Lizzie did a lot of swimming in the pond, which was chemically treated to control algae. I had a theory that there might have been some chemicals that she absorbed through her skin, and since she was pregnant, the chemicals could have affected the fetuses.

It was a shot in the dark, but still I wanted to test the pond water to see. But Lizzie's owners would not let me test the water. One of my clients, a scientist in Nevada, actually told me that I should sneak onto their property and take some of that pond water for testing, but I did not feel right about doing that.

Then Captain had another litter of puppies, and all the puppies died. That's when people really started screaming, and Captain's owner freaked out. Nobody had a clue what could have happened, and to be honest, neither did I. Since it was an entire litter, in my mind a genetic cause was still extremely remote. But by that time, many of our breeders had firmly decided that genes in the Captain line were going to be the ruin of the entire breed.

The Shiloh Shepherds AOL bulletin board was loaded with hysteria. Owners were panicked, and puppy buyers were confused. Many new breeders had no idea whom to listen to, and panic multiplied. My membership received anonymous mail-outs from one disgruntled person who was sure a genetic defect was to blame.

I tried to keep my mind clear so I could think of a logical solution.

I turned to a new theory. I remembered that when I was visiting Captain's owner she took me to a nearby farm and showed me a dog that looked just like Captain, on a chain at the farmhouse. The dog's mother was some kind of a husky-lab mix, yet she had a son that looked just like Captain! Hmmm. Captain's owner and I both figured that Captain must have snuck away from home and provided this little hussy with a free service. Since she only lived about a mile and a half down the road, it was a logical assumption. At the time it meant very little to either of us.

Then Pam McCloskey, another of my breeders who is also a scientist, hit upon something. She told me that what happened to those two litters of puppies sounded like canine brucellosis, which is a sexually transmitted disease. Captain could have contracted canine brucellosis from the farm dog, infected the second Captain/Lizzie litter, and deformed the puppies, because his sperm would have had defects. It could have killed the puppies in the third litter, which was born later, and then it would have made him sterile. Canine brucellosis is sort of like syphilis: it just gets progressively worse. We figured with him roaming around, he could easily have picked it up, if not from the

> **Canine Brucellosis**
> **By Pamela McCloskey**
>
> There is no greater tragedy for a dog breeder than to have a bitch abort or a male dog become infertile. Unfortunately, there is a disease that causes both abortions and sterility in dogs known as canine brucellosis.
>
> Canine brucellosis is a contagious bacterial infection of dogs caused by *Brucella canis*. It was first recognized in 1966, and its prevalence in dogs is probably as high now as when the disease was first discovered.
>
> *B. canis* infects a susceptible host by penetrating the mucous membranes of the oral cavity, vagina and conjunctiva. After infection, *B. canis* can be detected in the bloodstream within two to three weeks. This may last for six months, but it commonly persists longer than one to two years and has been observed as long as five years after infection. Brucellae localize in the lymph nodes, spleen, bone marrow, and reproductive tracts of males or gravid bitches.
>
> Infected, nonpregnant females are ususally asymptomatic, except for enlarged lymph nodes. Infected female dogs transmit *B. canis* only during estrus, at breeding or commonly following abortion at forty-five to fifty-five days of gestation. Early embryonic deaths and abortion two to three weeks after mating have been reported, but they are usually regarded as conception failures. Milk of infected bitches contains lower concentrations of bacteria and is less important in transmitting infection to surviving pups since most have already been infected in utero.

farm hussy, then from any of the other strays that he visited on his romantic escapades.

But by that time Captain's owner was not speaking to me, and she would not let us test Captain. She actually changed her phone number and hired lawyers, and said, "If you come near me, I'm going to sue all of you." She neutered Captain immediately, and she spayed the bitches in her kennel.

Hysteria was spreading out of control. At the time Captain was one of the finest dogs we had in our gene pool, but the owners of dogs who were related to him were so sure that they were carrying a genetic mutation that the majority of them neutered and spayed their dogs to prevent this supposed mutation from polluting the gene pool. This was done against my every wish.

I cried when I heard about some of our most magnificent dogs being neutered and spayed, out of pure ignorance, spurred on by outrageous gossip! All I could think of was the foolish reaction that some people had to the Orson Welles radio program "War of the Worlds," a fictional Martian invasion that caused people to flee New York, hide in cellars, load their guns, or even to wrap their heads in towels to avoid poisonous Martian gas.

Anonymous mailouts continued to accuse me of a horrendous cover-up. They said that the disease was spread throughout the gene pool, and they predicted that all the dogs were going to have it very soon. According to the rumors, this was nothing less than an epidemic.

I spent a lot of time answering accusations. My phone would start ringing at 7 a.m., and would not stop until well past midnight. I was starting to feel like a broken record, answering the same questions over and over again: "Let's give it some time, let's continue the research, let's find out what's really going on here, a genetic cause is highly unlikely." I couldn't get any water samples from the pond, and we couldn't test Captain, so all I could do was answer people's cruel accusations, and wait to see if any other Captain progeny got sick. It was a horrible time.

But after fourteen months of careful monitoring, not one of Captain's grandchildren showed any of the problems that had so cruelly affected that fateful litter. I relaxed a little. At least *my* dogs were surely okay! I sent a letter to the club membership, telling them that we could almost surely eliminate the possibility of a polygenetic threshold trait. No other dogs carrying most of the same genes, when inbred, outcrossed, or linebred, had shown any sign of this strange "back" problem.

But by then it was too late.

The reputation of the breed had been nearly ruined by the hysteria. Many people couldn't sell their puppies anymore because they were related to Captain or Lizzie. One crazy woman even started a fund for the Shiloh Shepherd victims, called the "Captain victims fund." People were sending her donations to prepare for future surgeries for all these nonexistent paraplegic dogs!

Not one pup was ever born with the defects found in that deformed litter. At this writing, ten years later, it has never happened. But that hysteria caused enormous destruction. We lost a lot of great dogs to the breeding program at that time. I still feel the pain of losing them. It took me nearly a decade to rebuild those lines.

Another casualty of all the hysteria was the Shiloh Shepherd Dog Club itself.

Captain descendents

GV Ch. Zion's A-Tribute to Snow's Grizz, OFA ROM

Ch Ptd. Trillium Adam Tribute to Zion, CGC TDI

"New" Club

With all the wars and battles going on—"flame wars" of verbal sparring on our Internet forums, rumors and innuendo in the club, anonymous mailouts—many people just got discouraged. A lot of good people walked away from the Shiloh Shepherd family during that time.

Unfortunately, some who stuck around were not the nicest people.

I got wind of a plan that was similar to those of my former vice presidents: If we can get rid of Tina telling us what to do, we can take off with this breed and make millions of dollars. In their eyes, I guess I was like the guard standing in front of Fort Knox.

Yes, I was controlling what my breeders were doing. I didn't apologize for that, because that was the whole idea. But they sure didn't like it. I told them, You can only breed a bitch once a year; you've got to wait until she's twenty-one months of age; breeding the bitch must cease when she is six years old. There were a lot of specific rules in place to protect the dogs' health and genes. But people would say things like, "My grandmother had a bitch on the farm that had twelve litters of puppies!" Basically, from their perspective, my rules were just hurting their income.

Then people started sending me hate mail.

It didn't hurt me much; it was just the next thing in a long line of hurtful actions. But I felt very betrayed. When you do so much for somebody, and they still hate you because you didn't give even more, you start thinking less of the human race. In the spring of 1996 I appointed a new vice president for the Shiloh Shepherd Dog Club, hoping that he would be able to deal with the complaints and discord.

Two of my more active members began running the club, saying that they would retain me as president as long as I was willing to act "properly." I was not comfortable with that term, but I wasn't really sure what they meant. Then they changed one of my letters to the membership without my consent, and I got the picture. I had been writing newsletters to my clients for over two decades, so being censored was a tough pill to swallow. Slowly, I realized that this new generation of members was asking me to be a different person. I chose to step aside, rather than compromise my principles.

Money was also an issue. At that time everyone knew that I was practically bankrupt, and I had told the breeders that I would stop funding advertising when the day arrived that I couldn't afford it; maybe this looming threat was making everyone hate me more. Then one of the men who was running the club for me basically said, "I've got lots of money. I'll tell you what, I'll carry all of you. Just follow me."

They started a new club, the International Shiloh Shepherd Dog Club, or ISSDC, in September of 1997, and I shut down the original Shiloh Shepherd Dog Club. I swallowed my pride and told them, "All right, I'll take a breather, you show me you can do a better job."

My efforts to maintain unity among the club members had failed. I was physically worn out, mentally drained, and financially busted.

The Fish Symbol

One of the major controversies about me and my leadership was my Christianity. Many people didn't like the fish being on the Shiloh Shepherd logo, and the leader of the new club had stated that the fish was one of the first changes on his agenda: According to him, Christian symbols did not belong in a dog club.

These dogs had been called "Shilohs" and carried the fish symbol since 1974. The fish had unequivocally been associated with the Shiloh name for over two decades. If you have read this far in my story, you know that I was only the servant of the real creator of the Shiloh Shepherd. I could not have created this breed by myself—I know because I tried. It was crucial to me that the breed be identified as God's creation.

When Christians were being persecuted by the Romans, the fish was a symbol of safety. When people were literally running for their lives, they would look for the fish symbol on a door, and that would tell them that it was a safe place to rest. The Greek word for fish, "ichthus," is an acrostic for Iesous (Jesus) CHristos (Christ) THeou (of God) Uiou (the Son) Soter (the Savior). During the Holocaust, when millions of Jews were taken to camps to be slaughtered, many German Christians painted the fish symbol on their doors to let the Jewish people know that here was a safe house. The small fish symbol in our breed logo does not state that the person owning a Shiloh is a Christian. It states only that this breed belongs to the Lord.

In July of 1997, there was a big meeting of the club at Grand Island in Buffalo. I rallied my troops, and the new leaders rallied theirs, and we all met to make a final determination about the future of the club.

Some people, even a few of differing ideologies, stood up and said, "The fish should not be removed. We should continue some of the foundations that Tina laid for the Shiloh Shepherd club, especially since this is so important to her." But others were not so nice. A woman I thought was a very good friend of mine for years went with the other club in the split. They were sitting at a table in the front of the meeting, the two ringleaders and my friend, and she was right in the middle. I listened as they tried to tell me that I should conform to their thinking, and encourage my loyal clients to join them, in order to strengthen their club.

I stood up and said, "I will tell you what. I will stand with your club as long as the fish stays, but if the fish goes, I go." And my former friend sat there with hatred in her eyes, and she took her little gavel and said, "Well, the fish has got to go," and banged the table.

I said, "Well, then, so do I, goodbye." I walked out of the room.

I felt like crying. About half the people in the room got up and left with me, and I did not plead for the people who stayed with the other club to come back.

New Registry and Response

In February, the "new" club announced that they would be forming their own registry. They even set up a new breed standard, which was a copy of mine with one change.

A breed standard is a blueprint of the breed it was written for; a guide for the judges to select dogs that conform "most closely" to the standard, and a tool for the breeders to help them determine the correct dogs that will improve the quality of future generations. The new club's "standard"—which they quickly revised back to our old standard—would have changed the guidelines for Shiloh rear angulation, making the dogs look much more like the modern German Shepherd than the very different kind of dog that we had been working towards for so long. That change may not seem like much to a novice, but, if implemented, it could have drastically altered the desired structure of our breed. If the new club wanted to breed dogs that looked like long-haired German Shepherds, why couldn't the members just breed long-haired German Shepherds, instead of trying to change the Shiloh?

My reply to their "new breed standard" was instantaneous. After contacting several of our members for advice, it was unanimously agreed that the SSDCA, Inc. needed to re-activate. For the sake of my dogs, and all of their faithful owners, I had to rebuild the club and finish the job I had started.

Not everyone agreed, and we suffered a great loss that year. Some people chose to stay with the new club, because their leader had convinced them that I would not be able to handle the financial burden. There were others who didn't want to stay with the new club, but were afraid that it would overpower me nevertheless, so they just chose to walk away.

I realized that my goal of finishing the breed was in jeopardy: The Shiloh Shepherd leaders were splitting up, and the gene pool was splitting up with them. Great dogs had been neutered in the "back issue" fiasco, and now many owners were leaving. Would I ever live to see the Shiloh Shepherd become a finished breed?

Broken-Hearted Breed Founder

To cheer myself up, I went off to a show in Heightstown, to see how the dogs were doing. During my drive, nostalgia flooded my soul. Images of the dogs I had seen at the Cherry Blossom Classic only three years ago nearly brought tears to my eyes.

SSDCA Newsletter Cover, 1997.

But as I sat ringside watching the Shilohs, a feeling of hopelessness overwhelmed me. I had been so busy dealing with the back issue and the ridiculous political wars, I didn't realize that the breed was really taking a beating. A new type of Shiloh seemed to be emerging, and it wasn't good. Most of the dogs in the ring that day should have been sold as pets. I realize that people love their pets, and think they are beautiful, but pets are not for the show ring. Those dogs barely made the minimum size requirements for Shiloh Shepherds. I saw Shilohs with hooked tails, with bitchy heads... In the traditional dog show world, many of them would have been laughed out of the ring.

I sat at ringside, feeling crushed. This was not what I had been working so hard to achieve! I certainly hadn't allowed myself to drift towards the edge of bankruptcy so that I could sit ringside and watch dogs I wasn't proud of.

Then slowly, a new feeling came over me. That show revived my spirit to go back out there and fight for the real Shiloh Shepherds, and the good breeders.

I thought to myself, There must still be a few good people left that feel the way I do, who will really look out for the future of these dogs! I need to find those special people who love this breed and will help me get them back to where they should be.

After that I picked myself back up and prepared to start over. I began by working in my own kennels.

Important Outcross

As I took a fresh look at my dogs, after so many months of political turmoil, I quickly realized that it was time to look for an outcross again. Every four or five generations you have to bring in new blood, or negative recessives will almost certainly pair up from too much inbreeding. I'd been so distracted by all the controversy, I'd nearly missed the window for outcrossing.

I had to find a dog that was compatible with the Shiloh Shepherd, a dog that would not compromise the quality that we had. Outcrossing is sort of like surgery: it's serious, but necessary to get rid of a problem. If I outcrossed quickly, I could still get in just in the nick of time, but I had to do it right. Our gene pool was already too small to survive if I made the wrong choice!

I knew about the Altdeutsche Schaeferhunde in Germany. They were farm-type, heavy-boned, easy-going, long-haired, old-style German Shepherds that had been growing in popularity as family companions and guide dogs in Europe. They were larger-boned and less high-strung than their typical "working" cousins. In the late '90s there was nothing about them on the Internet. I found all of my contacts via German magazines. I had long since lost all my German, so I had my mother make the phone calls. She loves to talk, and she proved to be an expensive intermediary!

In March of 1998 I brought Artus, an Altdeutsche Schaeferhunde, into the gene pool. I knew that wasn't going to be enough to get the job done, so

---

The Alt Deutscher Schaeferhunde (Old German Shepherd)

The long-haired Alt Deutsche Shaeferhunde comes from the Wurttenberger flock guardian dogs in Germany. The goal in breeding these dogs is for an alert, obedient companion, friendly with children. They can be trained as an obedience companion dog, Schutzhund, sport dog or as search and rescue, guiding eyes and therapy dogs.

Breeders must complete one year in a breeder's school prior to receiving permission to breed their dogs. They must be inspected by the breed warden within ten days of the litter being born and a second time after the puppies are tattooed. Each dog, prior to being bred, must qualify by meeting the structural requirements as per the breed standard, passing an endurance test, meeting size requirements, passing their hip x-ray, and being evaluated at a show and passing with no less than a good rating.

two years later I brought in Orbit, from the Hoofprint line. Joanne Chanyi, a phenomenal woman, developed the Hoofprint line of White German Shepherds. She's been breeding them since the mid-'60s and keeping explicit records. I was happy to have one of her dogs in the Shiloh pedigree, especially since he also carried the "real" Rin-Tin-Tin ancestors that have always impressed me! Thanks to that outcrossing, we had the best of the old movie/TV stars locked into our gene pool. I wanted our Shilohs to be known for their exceptional intelligence, and the Hoofprint line didn't let me down.

David and Artus   *Joanne Chanyi and Orbit*

> Joanne Chanyi of Hoofprint Kennels is a well-known and well-respected White Shepherd breeder. She began breeding White German Shepherds in 1968, with all dogs being x-rayed for hip dysplasia since 1975 and elbow dysplasia since 1991. Her data on any health concerns on her litters is exemplary. She has been actively involved with the White Shepherds Genetics project. Numerous Hoofprint dogs have gone on to become service dogs, performed Search and Rescue (SAR), and earned show and obedience titles. She is a founding member of the American White Shepherd Association and has been active in many other White Shepherd clubs and in the fight to allow White Shepherds in the CKC show ring. Hoofprint dogs may be found not only in Canada and the U.S., but also in Mexico, Germany, Switzerland, Cuba, France, Denmark, Germany, Holland, the Czech Republic, and Puerto Rico. In the White Shepherd Service Dog Hall of Fame, you will find the dogs that have made the greatest impact on this breed. Many proudly carry the Hoofprint name.

Getting back into the real business of dog breeding made me realize how insane all the "club wars" were. I decided to rise above politics: I would offer an amnesty to the breeders who had left during the former takeover attempt. I knew that many of them wanted to return to their commitment, so that we could rebuild our poor, battered gene pool and expand properly once more.

Barb Cullen, from Canada, and Mynde Bunker, from California, met with me in Niagara Falls and we formulated what we called the "Olive Branch Letter." Then Barb and Mynde contacted all former members and breeders with the new open invitation, while I worked feverishly to convince the SSDCA, Inc. board of directors to agree to this new amnesty proposal.

The board agreed to make some concessions, but they were not easy on the ones who came back. It was sort of like they were children: You ran away from home? Okay. You can come back home, but you're going to clean your room, and you're going to mop the floors! We made the rules very tough. They would be on a five-year probation, and we'd be watching to make sure they followed all the regulations. A few breeders came back in the amnesty, but the rest did not.

Then the door was closed.

New Lessons Learned

During those few intense years, I was surrounded by miracles. The late '90s were emotionally exhausting, but they also provided great blessings. There is no doubt in my heart, and there never has been, that God is in control! One thing I gained from those years was a new way of looking at myself. During our darkest hours, while the wars were raging, my pastor told me, "All your life you have expected instant obedience from your dogs, yet you are not willing to do as much for God!" That took a long time to sink in.

Then I realized that throughout all this controversy, I had been thinking too much about myself. My reputation. My finances. My dogs. But Matthew 6:19-34 says it best: *"Lay not up for yourselves treasures upon earth, where moth and rust doth corrupt, where thieves break through and steal. But lay up for yourselves treasures in heaven, where neither moth nor rust doth corrupt, and where thieves do not break through nor steal."*

Maybe my "treasures" weren't silver and gold; maybe they were the praise and glory I received from being the representative of these incredible dogs. I needed to let go of my vanity again. In a strange way, the worst of the crisis taught me how to relax.

In 1999, I placed a prayer request on my web site for strength. That Sunday in church, things I had underlined years ago in my Bible kept jumping out at me. "It's not by might, but by my spirit," says the Lord, "this mountain shall be removed."

I felt a total peace.

After I got home I received a phone call with some news: the "new" club was running into some internal conflicts of its own. The rocks were already starting to crumble, and I was overjoyed. But then I read Romans 12: 17-18: *"Recompense to no man evil for evil. Provide things honest in the sight of all men. If it be possible, as much as lieth in you, live peaceably with all men."*

I tried not to feel victorious that things were going badly for the new group, and instead concentrated on the things that were going well for me. I had my new blood, and the dogs were doing fine. I thought that I could happily kiss the heartbreaking 1990s goodbye.

But that was when I suffered the worst blow of all.

Chapter 7

Out of the Ashes

Remodeling

We had lived in the same house, on Shearing Road in Gainesville, New York, since 1978. As my kids grew older they took turns moving out and then moving in again; none of them ever wanted me to live alone. So when my son John moved out, Lisa decided to move back in with me in April of 1999.

I decided I was going to move into the upstairs, and Lisa and her boys would take the downstairs. I set up my office in what used to be my kids' playroom, where I could look out the window while I worked on my computer. I liked being able to see all the kennels, which were all around the house, and I had a bird's-eye view of the maternity ward and the puppy units.

Josh and David enjoy their final Christmas with Izzy.

In 1999 we did a lot of major remodeling. Lisa and I painted nearly all the rooms, and she even swirled the bathroom ceiling. She was extremely proud of her hard work. We got a new microwave, put in new kitchen cabinets, a new refrigerator, a living room set, carpeting, and a computer system for Lisa in the living room. In the main kitchen, we put in a bigger table and more chairs, and then we got the stove.

We had always used a woodstove to heat the house, but I had recently switched to a pellet stove, which was easier for me to operate alone. I decided to upgrade to a much bigger pellet stove when Lisa moved in, because I didn't want her two-year-old to get chilled after a bath, or even during some of our extremely cold nights. I had the new stove put in for Christmas, as my present to Lisa and the boys. It was top of the line. I purchased it from a local guy, who also installed it at a reduced fee.

Unfortunately, that stove was a big, big mistake.

Tuesday, January 25, 2000

There was a big brouhaha on the Shiloh Shepherd Internet forums, and I was getting tired of fighting these stupid controversies. I was constantly putting out "splinter fires," which was what we called AOL or bulletin board flame wars. In these "wars," someone, usually a Shiloh splinter group that had refused our amnesty offer, would start a topic having to do with the dogs, and it would end with people making personal attacks or telling lies. I tried to ignore them, but they frustrated me to no end, because they were damaging the reputation of the breed. A lot of the good guys wanted to just walk away from it and didn't want to be confrontational, but for me it was like, Yeah, right! These people are literally destroying our good reputation, and you're telling me to ignore them. I can't do that!

I was on the computer dealing with splinter fires for most of the day, and I was very tired, very fed up. I started reading my Bible. I had a report that I had to do for my church, an in-depth study of Exodus that my pastor had asked me to complete for him. I was working hard on it, and I had typed many pages of notes, but I had fallen behind in my work for the Lord because of all the splinter controversies.

Lisa was going into town to get groceries, and she knew how far I was behind in paperwork, so she offered to take both boys so I could work. Josh, my older grandson, did not want to go, so I said he could stay if he played quietly.

***

At four p.m., evening was coming on. I was upstairs in my room working, and Josh was playing.

My Exodus article was beginning to look better, when Josh began pestering me. He smelled dinner burning. I said, "Josh, dinner can't be burning. Your mother's not home yet, and when she gets home she's going to make dinner. She's at the store right now, don't interrupt me."

I was at my desk, still working on my report, and he started up again. So I said, "All right, Josh. Go downstairs, and whatever's burning, turn off the stove." He was six years old and not a stupid child, so I knew he could do that.

He started going downstairs, and he ran right back in again. He said, "The whole kitchen's full of smoke, Nana, do you really want me to go down there?"

Before I'd even stepped into the hall I could see that he was right. I grabbed Josh and Izzy, our house dog, ran down the stairs, and yelled for them to go outside. In the kitchen, the wall behind the new pellet stove was on fire. I saw the phone sitting on the table and I thought, Should I call 911? No.

I ran for the sink and I started filling a pot full of water, but while the pot was filling I was thinking, I'd better call 911. I called 911 and told them to hurry, I needed help—and then the phone died. The wires had burned through.

I turned off the stove and tried to throw water on the wall, but that wasn't doing anything. The smoke got worse. I opened the kitchen door to let the smoke out, and Josh was outside screaming about the puppies. So I started dragging the pups out of the house and placing them into the maternity ward runway. Josh held the gate as I carried each one out. I got Macho, and Lilly Bean, who was only about nine weeks old. It was freezing and snowy outside, so I had to stick her under my sweatshirt and run her out into the maternity ward.

We got all the house dogs out—except one.

When I got back from taking Lilly to the maternity ward, the entire back wall of the house was on fire. Josh was outside screaming for Izzy, his special friend, his caretaker dog. Just as I stomped through the snow to Josh, the whole back end of the house blew, with a huge explosion of flames. He started screaming "Izzy!"

Izzy had run back into the house to the boys' room. Why, I will never know. Maybe she wanted to protect her room? My eyes and throat felt like they were on fire. I ran back in and I tried calling her, but half the stairs were already burned. There was no way I could get to her.

At that moment Josh yelled to me that the firemen had come. When the first one got to us, I just sat down in the snow and begged him to do something. It was bitter cold, and I was shaking. I hadn't taken my boots or a jacket. Josh's brand new snowsuit he got for Christmas was hanging on the wall, but we never had time to grab it.

Josh was yelling at the fireman that his dog Izzy had run upstairs to hide. The fireman looked at the burning house, and then he looked at Josh. He said, "I'm sorry, but nobody's going back into that house, the house is ready to blow. I'm really sorry."

So we lost Izzy.

The cold was bone chilling. As evening came on, more and more fire trucks arrived. The temperature dipped into the single digits. One of the firefighters noticed that Josh was coughing heavily, and they ran all the way to the house with the stretcher. He was already going into hypothermia. He had just his house slippers on, and his jeans and his shirt, he didn't have a jacket on; he was just a little boy, shivering and scared. They wrapped him in a blanket and took him out on the stretcher to the ambulance.

Then another officer said that the kennel behind the house had dogs in it, so I ran to let Tammy and Tipper out—they were terrified. I got them in the training center and came back. Kit and Wolfie were in danger too, so I moved them. By then the entire house was in flames.

A window blew out in the maternity ward, and I was trying to patch the window because I had puppies in there, and there was no heat, because they had turned off the electricity. I concentrated on getting all that done, waiting for them to tell me what to do next.

That's when I discovered that the firemen couldn't even get the fire trucks across the bridge to our house. Our house was well off the road, down a path and over a bridge that crosses the East Koy Creek. The fire trucks on the scene could not cross the bridge without danger of getting stuck. Firefighters from seven companies arrived at the scene, but during the first half hour they could only do "damage control": keep the fire from spreading to the kennels, the maternity ward, the training center, and the barn. The house was now engulfed in flames.

I screamed at them to do something. They kept telling me there was nothing they could do, but I wouldn't believe it. I was frantic, yelling at the firefighters that they had to save it, everything I had was in that house! All I could do was stand there, helplessly watching as my room burned, thinking about my pictures, tapes and over three decades of nostalgia.

Within an hour, it was all gone forever.

Eventually the firemen were able to bring tow lines by pickup truck, and they pumped water out of trucks at the road and sent it down hoses to the house. But it was too little, too late. By that time the water that they were pumping in was not nearly enough to combat the huge fire.

Scott M. Vrooman Sr./Daily News

Out of control blaze
Firefighters from seven volunteer companies worked to contain this blaze Tuesday afternoon at 5015 Shearing Rd. more than half an hour after it started. A narrow bridge in the driveway prevented the larger fire trucks from getting to the house before it was destroyed.

Newspaper article: reprinted from the Warsaw Country Courier, *Thursday, January 27, 2000.*

The fire's aftermath.

I was shivering. They took me away to the bottom of the road, where the ambulance was. That was where I first saw Lisa, who was just standing there crying. When I saw her I said, "All of our paperwork, our pictures, everything—I watched it burn in front of my eyes!"

But Lisa hugged me and said, "Mom, you're still alive and so is my son, and that's all that matters."

Then she asked about our house dogs. I told her that I couldn't get Izzy to come down, and we all cried. Even the ambulance attendants did. A few weeks later, we discovered Izzy's bones in the ashes.

***

In the hospital all I could think of was last week's registry, which had not been processed yet, and the new membership applications that had been sitting on my desk. I had watched as my office burned and the flames shot out of the window. I was responsible to people. What would I do now?

I felt numb.

It was nearly midnight when I was finally dropped off at the motel room that the Red Cross had arranged for us. It was fourteen miles from the kennel. I could not stop thinking about all the dogs that were still sleeping out there, with no heat on that freezing night.

My son John had offered to let Josh and me stay with him, and Lisa and David could sleep on my mother's couch, but Lisa said no. She wanted us all together, even if we had to stay in a motel. She said that we were all she had left of her home now, just me and her sons.

She was right; family was literally all we had. I had no purse, no money, my cash was burned upstairs in my closet. We had no jackets, nothing. The first person that showed up at the motel room was Lyn Segee with a coat and a pair of gloves and a scarf for me. The Red Cross got diapers for the baby, and the drugstore in town opened up in the middle of the night and got all my meds for the next ten days, free of charge. After that, gifts and help from friends and neighbors started arriving in a steady stream. That stream never let up, even during my darkest moments.

Lisa and her husband Jamie drove back to the house that night. The firemen who were still working said there could be spark fires, and they were afraid that they could possibly spread to the kennels. But the firefighters were leaving, so Lisa and Jamie stayed all night, shoveling snow on the heap of ashes that used to be our house. I think Lisa was in shock. She never got back to the house until there was nothing left of it.

Meanwhile, I walked around the motel bathroom, pacing in circles. I didn't want to wake the boys up, so I walked around the bathroom. My mother had given Lisa a bathrobe and me a nightgown, because all I had was filthy clothes from the fire, but I was still cold.

I walked around in circles, wondering, now what. Now what?

At that point I was convinced that my dream for a new breed had ended. Crazy people had been literally torturing me, ruining my life for nearly ten years. I hadn't been spending time with the kids, I hadn't been spending enough time with the Lord, and now I had lost everything. Maybe it wasn't worth it. Maybe there shouldn't be a Shiloh Shepherd.

My house was mortgaged past what it was worth, I had used up all my credit cards, I had no insurance...

But what I kept thinking about was my pictures. My videotapes of Lisa when she was young; my boys on their first raft ride; Lisa at the horse show; Lisa and all her Shelties; the Homecomings. All the shelves had been full of pictures and videotapes—they were my memories. Now they had gone up in smoke.

After the Fire

The day after the fire there was a record-breaking snowstorm. A record-breaking snow in upstate New York is a really big snowstorm: many feet of snow. It was another burden piled on top of all our problems. All that snow, so much cold, and nobody to care for all those dogs.

I had stopped our home insurance in an attempt to save money, so we lost not only the house and all of its contents, we also found ourselves with a lot of extra expenses. The day after the fire we had seventy-eight dogs, plus young pups, at Shiloh Kennels with no water or electric. We had to find a way to keep them safe and warm.

I returned to the kennel for the first time the next morning as the snow was falling in heavy flakes. When I got there and saw the damage by daylight, all I could do was throw up. My son had to force me into his car and take me away from there.

I stopped at my mom's to make some calls to find somebody to ship the puppies out to their new homes. I was trying to focus on reality. Things had to be done. I called my friend Karen Ursel, and she asked about the dogs' health papers. I said they were done, and she could pick up copies at the vet. Then she asked about the shipping money, and I told her I had taken that out on Monday, so I could give Lisa the hundred-dollar bill for the vet and the rest was in my purse.

Then it hit me. I had left my purse in a closet for safekeeping. In my closet, at home. I broke into tears and had to put the phone down.

We set up shifts to go out to the property and care for the dogs. Lisa was usually the first one in at daybreak and always the last one out around midnight. Since it was the middle of winter, and we had extreme weather conditions, we had to bring fifty gallons of water out daily in jugs. We did this in three shifts because it froze so quickly in the sub-zero temperatures.

Several investigators came to inspect the damage, and their conclusions were the same: our new stove had been installed with the wrong kind of pipe, and that was what burned the house down.

We were all emotionally devastated, but slowly we moved forward. Karen's husband brought down a generator so we would have some power at the kennel. We hired out extra help to care for the dogs. The emotional and financial support we received from our friends and neighbors kept us pushing forward, despite unbelievable odds.

But I felt dazed, day and night.

***

Lisa had been staying at the kennels every night until nearly 1 a.m., and then she had to get up at 6 to get the boys ready for school. I could not sleep, and I could not eat. I felt like I was useless.

On the third night I told Lisa that I would drive the kids to school so she could get a little bit of sleep. But the next morning when I went to start the car, I realized that my glasses had been on top of the computer desk, in my office, at home.

I felt sick again. I can't drive without my glasses; anything more than ten feet away is a blur. I couldn't risk going nearly twenty miles without being able to see, so I had to wake Lisa up. I had always carried the load, but this load was just too heavy.

Lisa and my sons were carrying me.

As I waited for Lisa to return from her shifts at the kennel, I read the letters that Shiloh dog owners were sending me for support. Karen Ursel, my friend and the administrator of our website, had been printing them off for me and then faithfully bringing them to the motel for me to read. Those letters contained so many prayers and so much concern. I was in shock, but the letters gave me moments of sanity. They made me feel less alone.

Those first few nights in the motel, Lisa and I did a lot of soul searching. We both knew that we had to stay on track with the Lord, no matter what. Whatever I found during my daily studies that encouraged us, we would just cling to like a life raft. I remember in particular finding Isaiah 54: 7-8, which says: *"For a small moment have I forsaken thee; but with great mercies will I gather thee. In a little wrath I hid my face from thee for a moment; but with everlasting kindness will I have mercy on thee, saith the Lord thy redeemer."*

Starting Again

After a few days, I finally gained the ability to focus on the dogs and ignore the remains of the house. Paying attention to the dogs kept my mind occupied long enough to get a few things done.

Lisa and Jamie, my sons Richard and John, and Marc and Lyn Segee removed the top floor rubble, piece by piece, looking for anything that could possibly be saved. They picked through the charred, soaked, frozen remains of the house, but most things were destroyed beyond recognition. Lisa proudly announced that she had located the firesafe ISSR filing cabinet. That made me feel better, but then I thought of the papers that had not been processed yet, that had been in the "in" box on top of the files, and I felt sick to my stomach again.

Then we found something that looked like it might be the hard drive of Lisa's computer, and my heart leapt. Could some of our data be saved? But it turned out to be part of the copier—everything was so charred and melted, it was impossible to tell one thing from another.

We went through the last of the rubble. Although Lisa's room, which was on the far corner of the house, suffered a lot of damage, one old dresser was still standing. In the bottom drawers, a few memories—only a bit charred—still survived. There was a picture of Shep and Lisa at the carnival in 1992. It was strange how such small, silly things could bring us so much joy. The fireproof files were partly destroyed, but when we found a tiny key chain that held a picture of Josh when he was born, and was only slightly burned, we rejoiced.

We moved forward slowly. Karen took me to the Red Cross and they took care of getting my glasses replaced, and I started communicating with other friends through her.

I was recovering my abilities, but looking into the future was still too hard to do.

Standing at the Crossroads

I have always been a hard worker. If something needed to be taken care of, I would just work harder until it got done. In this case, I just didn't know where to begin. I knew that we needed to find a place to stay, and we needed to make plans for a future, but I couldn't think about it. Some choices in our near future would be difficult, and some would be beyond difficult.

I didn't understand what God was telling me. Was He telling me to stop breeding dogs? If the fire was the only way He could get me to let go of them, and that's what He really wanted, well... maybe I'd better let go of them.

The more I thought about it, the more certain I was that God must want me to stop breeding Shiloh Shepherds. What else could all of this mean?

Every night Lisa and I talked well into the night in our motel room, searching for answers but not finding many. I was still not able to sleep more than a few hours each night, and I could not hold down much food. I decided to try something; maybe it would give me a clue about what the Lord wanted.

I called Matthews, who was the director of Kirby Vacuum Cleaners in Rochester, and said, "Okay here's the scoop. I'm flat broke, my house has burned down, I've got nothing left. I'm ready to move back to Rochester. What kind of deal can you offer me? Find me a house, I'll take whatever, I'll go back to working for Kirby."

Matthews gave me a good offer. I could train new salespeople, I could make a steady paycheck. We could make it, and my family was going to be okay. I'd just have to give up the dogs.

All I had to do was let go of the dogs.

Re-Homing My Dogs

One of the first things we had to do was place as many of our dogs as we could part with into good homes ASAP. I sent out pleas for homes through our website and through the club, and lots of people wanted them. We had more offers than we had dogs; in the first month alone we placed twenty-two.

But I still ended up holding onto fifty-four dogs.

I know it sounds crazy to keep fifty-four dogs if you have nowhere to keep them, but I hadn't entirely decided if I really was going to abandon the breed. Lisa and I made out a list, keeping only those that had to stay in order for the breed to survive; those dogs represented the heart of the gene pool. If I gave them up, my dream for the Shiloh Shepherd would officially end. I had to keep them just until I was sure what I should do.

Goldie, one of my dogs, was due to give birth the week of the fire. My friend Lyn Segee took Goldie and whelped her for me. If she hadn't, if Goldie had stayed out in the maternity ward without any help, I'm sure she would have lost the whole litter. Karen did the same for a dog named Eve.

When Goldie's puppies were born, I went and visited them. They were adorable and showed so much personality. Seeing them was the first thing that felt good in a long time. The pups I evaluated were getting fat and sassy, and one silly pup even brought a smile to my face. Those pups would someday make their mark on the future Shiloh world.

Mygic's birth was one of the many blessings that I rejoiced over. If Goldie had stayed at the farm, he may have never survived, but the Lord provided a safe place for her to whelp this magnificent white giant!

When I did the Litter Evaluation on this litter, I knew he was special and his progeny would someday make a large impact on our gene pool. By the time he was just a yearling he had already exceeded my wildest expectations, and now that he has matured I think he is a magnificent representative for our breed. But even more important than that is the fact that he has been able to produce the quality we so desperately need in all future Shiloh Shepherds.

If there was a future Shiloh world...

The more I tried not to think about the future, the more I began to nurture secret hope for my dogs. I couldn't help but notice that many of the people who adopted dogs as a result of my tragedy were good, caring people, with real respect for the breed. Many of them were Christians. Was it possible that doors were opening in ways I had never anticipated? Would I keep on meeting future breeders like Dawn Swick, who adopted my Vicky and fell so deeply in love with the breed that she now has eighteen Shilohs in her kennel? By losing everything, and even giving away so many of my dogs, was I finally gaining the kind of breeders I'd been looking for?

It's amazing how I can look back now and see what the Lord had in mind for me. But when I was still in the midst of the storm I didn't let my hopes get too high. I said, "Okay, Lord, you open the doors, I'll walk through them. Otherwise I'm not going anywhere."

Recovering Our Records

My computers were not salvageable—they had melted into nothing. The top floor of my house fell onto the bottom one; everything in between was destroyed. Since I had spent most of my life doing things the old-fashioned way, I'd kept all of my paper records, dating back for over thirty years, in my house. Knowing they were gone felt like someone had reached in and pulled my heart out. For so many years I had been so proud of my record-keeping; it had been a real anchor in my life.

I no longer had the breeder's books that I had kept for all those years. I spent a lot of time beating myself up for not keeping them in a very expensive fireproof safe. I had to swallow my pride and send a general letter to the club, asking these people to please re-send us copies of their records so that we could rebuild our files.

Like my pictures, my records represented my past, my memories. Losing them was extremely painful. I was getting to the point where I was okay in the present, and I could almost think about the future, but thinking about the past made me feel like an elephant was sitting on my chest. Often I could hardly breathe.

One thing that kept me together was that I knew that the Shiloh Shepherd registry records, which are stored in triplicate in Texas at TCCP, were safe.

Stephen Betcher always demanded a ten-day turnover of information from me to him. He was kind of a slave driver! At least twice a month, he wanted those packets or we got a nasty phone call—"Assume the position, I don't have my packet here! What's your problem!" But since he was so tough on us, there was almost no amount of data loss of any kind. Litter papers, registration papers, whatever, he had complete data.

If Stephen and Barbara Betcher had not kept such perfect records for the ISSR all of these years, I would not have been able to survive emotionally, and I owe them my most sincere thanks.

The Barber Fund

One day Karen Ursel told me, "I got a call from Barb and Dave Cullen, your clients, from Canada. And they want to talk to you." Then she drove me up to Ontario, Canada. When we got there a bunch of people were there who had pooled their resources, and they said, "We're going to loan you the funds that you need to set up another kennel so that you can keep your dream going."

I was really touched. But at that time I was just so tired, and I couldn't think about my future. I said, "Thank you so much. But I'm not going to keep going. I'm tired of fighting. I just don't want to keep going."

And we turned around and went home.

Storm and Jena, owned by Barb and Dave Cullen.

Urgent Notice: SSDCA Advisory Board Letter

Your immediate attention and cooperation is needed regarding a terrible tragedy which has occurred regarding the founder of the Shiloh Shepherds, Tina Barber, and her family!

While we sit comfortable in our heated or air-conditioned homes, looking at our Shiloh Shepherds or pictures of them, please think about the Barbers. Their kennels now sit next to a burned wreck of a house whose smoldering embers have been slowly extinguished by the snow that has fallen. All extra monies for many years were poured back into helping this breed become the dogs that we love and adore today. Because of this there is no money for rebuilding her home.

There is no longer a place to stay on the property. The dogs in Zion Kennels are all relatives of our dogs, from the past, for the present and into the future. For the Shiloh Shepherd future to continue we are asking for your personal help. Help to rebuild a bridge. Help to rebuild a home. Both of these are important to the future of the Shiloh Shepherd. It will be through your help that the bridge to continue to the future is accomplished. Let's keep Tina's dream alive and help her in her time of need. Everything the Barbers owned will need to be replaced. Things that we take for granted such as the glasses we drink from, the shampoo for our hair, the towels we dry ourselves with, the socks for our feet—all are gone.

Those who have experienced this kind of loss know it is not easy to recover quickly. It takes time, and most of all, it takes money.

Please consider donating whatever money you possibly can to the Barber Fund. Whether it is a $5, $50, or $500 donation, every bit helps. There are over 250 SSDCA members and over 2000 Shiloh Shepherd owners. Just think of what we can do if we all contribute something. First, this fund will be used to provide housing for Tina, Lisa, Josh and David as soon as is humanly possible. Second, any extra money will cover the cost of setting up housekeeping again and purchasing supplies for the kennel. Contributions made by check or money order should be made out to the SSDCA, Inc. with a notation at the bottom that it is to be used for "The Barber Fund."

A listing of all donors will be printed in the next newsletter.

Thank you for your support.

The SSDCA Advisory Board

Pam Dymond-Weed

Pam McCloskey

Billy Pellicane

Lyn Segee

Karen Ursel

Pat Urso

However, they would not take "no" for an answer. They wanted me to find another place and start rebuilding because they did not want to see the breed end like this. I recall Billy Pellicane, whom I'd affectionately called "Brooklyn Billy" from the first day I met him, even before he got his "Warba," CH Bionic Snow Warrior of Zion, telling me that I couldn't give up on these dogs, because he wanted to make sure that if he ever had grandkids, even twenty years from now, they would not have to be deprived of experiencing the companionship of a real Shiloh Shepherd.

By that time Karen had also organized the Barber fund and the Tina fund. She was on the Internet organizing forums, rallying all the troops, doing everything one human being could possibly do to help me and my family. She would call me on the phone and tell me what everybody on the Internet was saying, and I would tell her what I had to say, and she would post it for me.

And the donations poured in.

Within ten days, fourteen thousand dollars came in for the Tina fund, which was for emergency supplies. An additional $36,000 was raised for the Barber House fund by July of 2000.

I knew that I had the motel from the Red Cross for only two weeks, but I hadn't been able to think beyond that. But with the offer of the loan from the Cullens, and all the money pouring in, and the people writing or e-mailing their support and love—it was amazing. I gathered some strength. It was like I opened my eyes for the first time since the fire.

When we picked up our mail in Gainesville, we always found special cards and letters that my Shiloh family was sending. Many included encouraging quotes from the scriptures. Not a day went by that my box was empty. Even if some only sent out an occasional card, Corinne did not fail to send them daily. Those cards and letters never failed to encourage us to stay focused on the positive. I quickly found an apartment close to the kennels, so we could go back and forth and take care of the dogs. Computers and fax machines were donated. Furniture was donated. My church brought three bedroom sets: beds for the boys, dressers, a bedroom set for me, a bedroom set for Lisa. They donated a living room set, two television sets, a washer and dryer... everything. And then out of the Tina fund I bought sheets, a vacuum cleaner, towels, and basic necessities to keep us going. The rest was used to maintain the dog care back at Shiloh Kennels.

I think Josh, my grandson who lived through the fire with me, was very traumatized by it. Once we got into our new apartment, he would walk around smelling things, checking the radiators—the fire really scared him.

It scared me too. I don't know if I will ever truly get over what I lost. But some of the things the fire gave me I would never want to give back.

New Lessons Learned

There are some good people left in this world. Believe me, shortly before the fire, I had given up on the human race. I hated people. But the Lord wanted me to set my priorities straight. I was so busy fighting, it was almost like, Step back, Tina, that's enough.

Yes, the Lord had been preparing me for this. Even through the most incredible hardship, my family was safe, all of the pedigree data was safe, many pictures had been saved via our website, and all of the dogs were safe. It taught me to keep my focus on what was left, not on what was lost. And it taught me to value the wonderful people I had met over the years, people who truly cared.

So many people came to my aid, it made me realize that the bitterness of a few was overshadowed by the goodness of so many others. I was flooded with letters, cards, and e-mails. Against my better judgment, I felt renewed hope for the breed. Could it be that God had been preserving the Shiloh Shepherd through people like Stephen and Karen without my even realizing it? I had suffered through my tragedy, but maybe—with the influx of good people coming to my aid—the breed would actually be better for it!

I still wasn't sure. Maybe God was using the fire to tell me that I should sell vacuum cleaners for a living.

But by this point I hoped that maybe He wasn't.

Renewed Hope

A few of my friends, Karen, Lyn, and Corinne, kept looking for a place for me to move to permanently. They all went into a mass search, calling realtors, and I didn't have anything to do with it; a big part of me still thought I was probably going to be moving back to Rochester.

I was looking at things realistically. Since the small insurance policy I had on the Shearing Road property went to the mortgage holders, and rebuilding would be out of the question due to various zoning difficulties, my only choice was to find a house and build kennels from scratch. But how could I? I was bankrupt. The properties available were much too expensive, and the kennels would be way beyond my reach.

As my friends went looking for potential houses, they soon discovered that my pessimism was correct. It was impossible. Even thirty-six thousand dollars was not going to be enough to get a house. No way. Not to mention the cost of constructing proper kennels, a whelping room, and other necessities for all those dogs! It would easily take ten times that amount.

I waited to see what the Lord would do, but I didn't let myself get too hopeful.

In April my pastor shared a word of prophecy in church. He assured me that the Lord was still in control, and had not forsaken the Shilohs. He had made plans for me for a blessing, not a curse:

> **Isaiah 51:11:** *Therefore the redeemed of the Lord shall return, and come with singing unto Zion; and everlasting joy shall be upon their head: they shall obtain gladness and joy; and sorrow and mourning shall flee away.*
>
> **Isaiah 52:6-7:** *Therefore my people shall know my name: therefore they shall know in that day that I am he that doth speak: behold, it is I. How beautiful upon the mountains are the feet of him that bringeth good tidings, that publisheth peace; that bringeth good tidings of good, that publisheth salvation; that saith unto Zion, Thy God reigneth!*
>
> **Isaiah 54:10-17:** *For the mountains shall depart, and the hills be removed; but my kindness shall not depart from thee, neither shall the covenant of my peace be removed, saith the Lord that hath mercy on thee. O thou afflicted, tossed with tempest, and not comforted, behold, I will lay thy stones with fair colors, and lay thy foundations with sapphires. And I will make thy windows of agates, and thy gates of carbuncles, and all thy borders of pleasant stones. And all thy children shall be taught of the Lord; and great shall be the peace of thy children. In righteousness shalt thou be established: thou shalt be far from oppression; for thou shalt not fear: and from terror; for it shall not come near thee. Behold, they shall surely gather together, but not by me: whosoever shall gather together against thee shall fall for thy sake. Behold, I have created the smith that bloweth the coals in the fire, and that bringeth forth an instrument for his work; and I have created the waster to destroy. No weapon that is formed against thee shall prosper; and every tongue that shall rise against thee in judgment thou shalt condemn. This is the heritage of the servants of the Lord, and their righteousness is of me, saith the Lord.*

Then on April 19th, a realtor called me and said, "There's a house available. It's a real bargain, because their realtor told the sellers their house was a white elephant and it would never sell." I asked her why it was so cheap, and she said, "The sellers have been Newfoundland breeders for twenty years. There are big dog kennels all over the property." My heart stopped. Could this be the place the Lord had prepared for the Shiloh Shepherd?

New Zion

Chapter 8

Old Friends, New Beginnings

Walking Without a Flashlight

Lisa and I struggled through each month, trying to stay faithful. Small miracles kept us going, even when we had nothing else. It was in April that the realtor located the former home of the Newfoundland breeders. That house was much smaller than my old place; if we got it, we would be able to have only about a third of the dogs we were used to. But finding it made me feel that if we could get it, then maybe I wasn't supposed to give up my dogs after all—and that thought made me happy. We named the place "New Zion."

I forfeited our destroyed house in June, because I had nothing left to pay the remainder of the mortgage. That wrecked the one thing I had left to my name—my credit. The bank gave me a letter stating that all the animals had to be out of the kennels and off my old property by the end of May, but I had no idea where I was going to put so many dogs. We put an offer on New Zion, and it was accepted, but getting a mortgage takes time.

The bank was about to auction off my old property, and I still hadn't found an appropriate place for the dogs. In desperation, I contacted them for an extension. They said, "No, sorry, we're auctioning the property off." At that time I had twenty-eight dogs still living there.

But the next day I got a call from the bank manager. She said, "I talked to the board, and we're going to extend you until the end of July." That was one of my little miracles. They postponed their auction by almost two months. Meanwhile, I waited for mortgage confirmation for New Zion. And waited and waited...

I knew the Lord was leading, but I couldn't see the next step in front of me. It was like walking in the woods at night without a flashlight; I just had to keep walking. I had a lot of support, and people were trying to help, but I had no security, no stability, no income, no possessions, and now no credit. The only thing that would get me into New Zion was a miracle. Walking by faith is very difficult to do. People always talk about it, but if you're actually forced into doing it, it will shake you to your roots.

The whole month of August was totally up in the air. Mr. Link, the owner of New Zion, let me use the kennels there to board my dogs, with the understanding that I was going to buy the property. The deposit for the closing had been raised, all the requirements had been met, and I had set up the phone, electric, garbage, and propane accounts in my name. All we had to do was receive a final mortgage commitment and close. Homecoming was fast approaching, invitations had already been mailed, and we had to get final preparations made.

The next day, I got a failure notice on the mortgage.

The bank would not fulfill their mortgage commitment because it was a "dual purpose" property, with more than 25% of the home designated for commercial use. Another lender offered a loan at 18% interest, which was not even an option. Eighteen percent interest is like buying a house on credit cards! There was no way I could pay it, especially since I would be cutting my stock down to a third. I felt that the door to New Zion had closed. All my hopes were devastated.

Prior to the fire, if I wanted something and I didn't get it, I could say, Well, I guess the Lord didn't want me to go in that direction. I didn't feel deprived, because I knew He always provided for my needs, and a little extra. After the fire it was different. I felt like, I need this! Why aren't You giving it to me?

Before the fire, if I needed more, I could just work harder. But after it, my sense of control was pulled away from me. I tried to let go and trust God to give us what we needed, but it was so hard. I couldn't help worrying. What if I ask Him for what I need, and He says no?

We tried to locate private financing for New Zion, but with such a short notice, that failed too. As Homecoming started, we received an eviction notice giving us ten days to remove all of our dogs from the New Zion property. We'd already given notice on the apartment, so I had to move out of there. Suddenly, I had nowhere to go. We'd invited people for Homecoming on the New Zion property, and they were coming. We had nowhere to put them.

A Tense Homecoming

In desperation I contacted Woodstream, a campsite in Gainesville, and said, "Listen. We've got no place for Homecoming, I don't even have a place to live. But every year we've had a Homecoming, we haven't failed since 1974. It's last minute, but can we hold it at your place?"

They said yes, and we rushed to let everybody know where Homecoming was going to be.

In the end, Homecoming came off very nicely. Pam Dymond-Weed came from Seattle in her big motor home, set up camp, and helped set up the ring. We had over fifty people at Homecoming, and everyone was supportive and wonderful. My friends carried me through it. Everybody pitched in.

I've always been the one in charge of Homecoming. I'm the hostess, so I make all the arrangements. "Here's where you put the ring, here's where you put the tents. Yes, Lisa's got to get her table set up over here. Do you have this? Do you have that? Where are the badges? Who brought the badges?" I'm nuts the day before Homecoming trying to get stuff together.

That year I didn't do anything. I spent my time sitting at a picnic table, talking to different people, playing with the dogs—I didn't take on any responsibility, it was just taken away from me and they ran with it. I enjoyed being a participant, and I felt at peace. At Homecoming I shared my frustrations with a lot of people, and everybody kept telling me that they were all praying about housing for me and my dogs. Many people said they knew the Lord was going to open a door soon.

They were right.

Tina admires a very special gift from two of her loyal friends, Corinne Filipski and Pam Dymond-Weed. It is a special Serenity Prayer plaque, which reads:

> *God grant me*
> *the Courage to change*
> *the things I can change,*
> *The Serenity to accept those*
> *I cannot change,*
> *And the Wisdom to know*
> *the difference.*
> *But God, grant me the courage,*
> *not to give up*
> *on what I think is right even though*
> *I think it is hopeless.*

Just after the Homecoming, I got a call from Mr. Link, the property owner. They had decided to lease the New Zion parcel to me for a year, with minimal interest, to give me an opportunity to get myself established. After a year, when my credit was back on track, I could get a mortgage that I could afford. We met at his lawyer's office, made all the agreements, went out to lunch, came back and signed the papers. It all happened in about four hours.

Then we moved onto the property. After seven months of living apart from my dogs, we were all back together at last! We quickly set up the place with donated furniture, and then rolled up our sleeves and got to work. We had seven litters during the fall of 2000. Our rebuilding was underway.

New Zion was literally a new beginning for me.

New Tools

To get my mind back into business, I started working on pedigree research on my donated kitchen table at New Zion.

Back in the mid-'90s I had been seeking the answer to why esophageal achalasia had mysteriously reemerged in our gene pool, after it had been wiped out for nearly fifteen years. I had not gotten very far with my pencil and calculator, and I had even called an expert geneticist to look at the data with me. We both ran into dead ends.

After a lot of effort, in the late '90s another expert geneticist recommended that I try a commercially available computer program designed by the late Larry Ritter of RCI Software to determine the relationship coefficient. The RC program calculates exactly how closely related two dogs in a breeding program are to each other. Dr. John B. Armstrong of the University of Ottawa and Dr. Jerold S. Bell of Tufts University School of Veterinary Medicine used it to find out what was causing some surprising genetic problems in dogs. I purchased the commercial version in late 1998 and we immediately merged in our ISSR data from the TCCP program in order to run thirty generation reports. Right away those reports gave me surprising new insights into what was happening in our gene pool.

Here's how the program works: When dogs are closely bred, certain ancestors way back in the pedigree can show up so many times on the family tree that those long-gone dogs can actually greatly affect the genetic makeup of a puppy. This kind of thing is nearly impossible to predict through regular pedigree research, but the RC program instantly tells you if there are any past-generation dogs that are pulling more weight than they should.

Why do we care? Because if those relationship coefficient numbers are too high, you've got dogs that are too closely related, and that can mean big problems. As I started to re-build my lines yet again, I knew that I didn't have any time for mistakes. I did a careful study of the RCs for each potential pairing.

Inbreeding is dangerous, everybody knows that. But many breeders thought that line breeding, which is nothing less than a watered-down version of inbreeding, was always safe. That's why everyone was surprised when unexpected problems popped up, even among strict line-breeders: Dalmatians developed problems with deafness, and then there was the collie eye problem, etc.

By unknowingly breeding a pair with a high relationship coefficient, breeders had been compounding a gene that had been floating around. The process was akin to a hair that starts a clog by pulling more things to it, and then before you know it, that one hair has plugged up the whole sink. That's genetic overload. All of these new health issues were arising due to condensed gene pools.

I spent countless hours researching the Shiloh Shepherd gene pools in light of all the new information the RC program gave me. Even though I personally knew all of the dogs used in the development of the Shiloh, and I could easily write pedigrees on nearly any registered dog for up to nine generations, I was amazed at some of my discoveries. I started running relationship coefficient reports and saying, "Ah, I see." For some past breedings I could see numeric evidence that we shouldn't have made the choices that we did. I ran RCs for some of the breedings we had done before I brought in Artus and Orbit as outcrosses in the late '90s, and I was floored by the numbers. One of them was 44 percent!

We had thought that those dogs were not closely related enough to be a genetically dangerous match, but the dogs in their backgrounds told a whole different story. As I planned for our next expansion, the RC program gave me much more confidence about making good matches. And then another good tool came my way.

Shortly after I moved into New Zion in 2000, my friend Joanne Chanyi told me about something she had been doing with her American White Shepherds called a health survey. I thought it was a marvelous thing. The health survey helped to determine the probable outcome of breeding particular carriers for different diseases. Joanne hooked me up with Dr. George Padgett, of Michigan State University, and the author of *Control of Canine Genetic Diseases*, and he agreed to do the health survey for the Shiloh Shepherd.

Our goal with the health survey was to identify genetic problems, and to track the individual dogs that had been passing them on, so that their progeny could be monitored for the welfare of future generations. Thanks to the tireless efforts of our Genetic Task Force, in particular Pat Urso, who called hundreds of owners encouraging them to participate, we were able to collect a large number of reports for the survey. Our survey results indicated that, other than pano and umbilical hernias, the largest percentage of diseases fell into the immune deficiency category, related to over-inbreeding. We have seen a lower incidence of immune deficiency diseases as our RCs have decreased.

The progeny from the outcrosses to Artus and Orbit were not included in the original survey, but we have continued to track data through our ongoing online health survey. We now maintain a disease database, thanks to the efforts of Debbie Knatz, as well as those of other Genetic Task Force members and licensed breeders. All of this makes breeding much safer than it ever has been. The tools available to breeders now have come a long way in the forty years of my experience.

As I continued my planning and pedigree research with the RC program and the health survey, I had more power and knowledge than ever, and I was feeling confident. The "splinter wars" were behind me. I'd just overcome a huge tragedy, I had a new kennel going, and I now had great new tools at my fingertips. I thought the final ten years to finishing the breed would go like clockwork.

I was wrong.

Almost Famous

A Shiloh Shepherd owner who worked at a big movie studio in Canada called me one day. She said that she had a couple of producers who were possibly interested in shooting a documentary on Shiloh Shepherds and New Zion. She called it "Birth of a Breed." She actually put up a website for the documentary, and started doing major promos for it.

That was like a blast of adrenaline for me. We were finally being recognized. The Shiloh was going to make it, the breed was going to move forward, everything was going to be okay!

The documentary started with interviews, and then for Homecoming 2001, which was filmed, we decided to splurge. We invited the three top judges in the country—Don Robinder, Fran Attridge, and Fred Lanting—as well as George Padgett, the top geneticist in the country. It was a big to-do.

Then for the next eight months, Karen and I went up to Canada to work on the film on weekends. We dug out pictures, data, and health survey reports. Many people in our organization, including myself, put a lot of time and money into the project. I spent hours and hours marking footage, doing outlines, and putting together layouts. By April, we were all ready to roll with the documentary. That's when all hell broke loose.

The filmmaker called me again. She said that the producer had gotten some bad vibes—he had heard that the Shiloh was not really a breed of dog, but rather a wolf hybrid. I had no idea what in the world she was talking about.

Evidently some people from the Shiloh splinter groups had been spreading rumors on the Internet to discourage the producers from completing the documentary. They were saying that some of our dogs had wolf in them, but that had never been exposed, and there could be lawsuits: The producer would be liable for putting together a documentary about a breed of dog that was really a con act—a bunch of wolf hybrids passing themselves off as a real breed!

I was horrified. I knew that the splinter groups didn't like me, but this was *ridiculous*. Didn't they know I'd just lost everything? And didn't they realize that they were also slandering their own dogs? I could not believe that even those people could stoop so low.

Then they stooped lower.

Some of the same people began posting fake documentation on the Internet to show that the Shiloh was actually developed from nothing but wolves. According to this "documentation," I had been continually putting wolf in secretly, faking papers to make it look like the Shilohs were dogs instead of wolves!

The Shiloh Shepherd Yahoo group forums became scary places to visit, full of controversy. After a while I was able to discern a pattern: Somebody from a splinter group would write in with a fake name, and say that they had a friend (who didn't want to be named), and their friend had some piece of damning information about me. One claimed to have pictures of the wolves that I was hiding behind my barn. Another one said, There's a new DNA test coming out; if somebody points out that your dog is a Shiloh, and the authorities want to have him tested, they can confiscate your dog!

It was insane stuff. But producers scare easily, and that was enough to put an end to that project. They pulled the plug on the documentary, and all of our investments of time and money went right down the drain.

Ridiculous. But boy, did it hurt.

All dogs are related to the wolf at one point. (Of course, that includes even the Chihuahua!) The German Shepherd was created with wolf in it; Max von Stephanitz used several different wolf varieties, it's documented in the

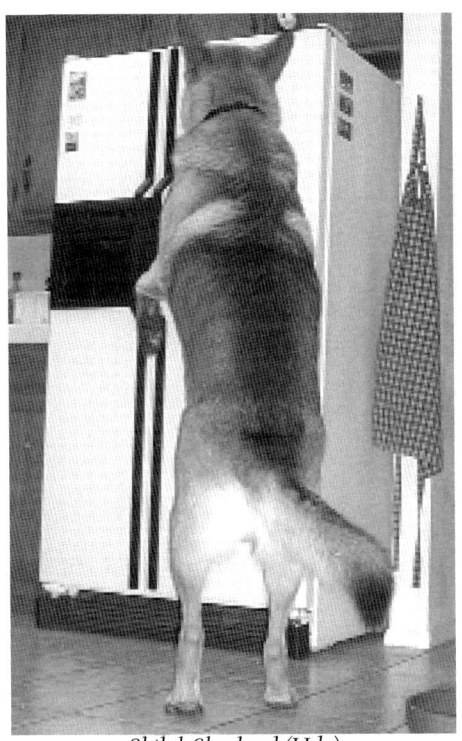

Shiloh Shepherd (Udo):
"Where are my chicken wings?"

pedigrees and in the stud books, so it's no secret.

But the wolf is so far back in any dog's gene pool that it really doesn't affect the dogs. I believe that some dogs that have a higher link to the wolf are more intelligent dogs; for example, some German Shepherds have more wolfish ancestry than others, and that's what I consciously pulled through our gene pool. The stronger wolf aspect is one of the reasons we have the better hips, and such amazing intelligence. The recently FCI-recognized Ceskolensky Vlcak is a beautiful creature that is known for its outstanding loyalty, and extreme intelligence—not to mention its rock-solid constitution. Very few health problems have ever been reported in these dogs because of the focus of their founder, Karel Hartl, on producing only stock with an extremely strong immune system. Many varieties of dogs have wolf that can be traced somewhere back in their genes.

But Shiloh Shepherds are certainly not wolves.

I was devastated by the loss of the documentary. And I was mystified by the splinter groups' relentless desire to attack me. If I'd been driving on bald tires on an icy road at eighty miles an hour, and I crashed my car, I could look at it and say, Well, that's why it crashed! But I was unable to analyze why we'd lost the documentary. It seemed like complete nonsense.

At length, I realized that it must all be about money again. There was a lot of talk on the Internet about Shiloh registries, which ones were legitimate, and which were not. I had been posting everywhere that our registry, the ISSR, had over forty years' worth of pedigrees, and contained detailed records for over 4,000 separate dogs. I told everyone who would listen that most of the other "registries" averaged between twenty and one hundred dogs, and were brand new. My actions probably caused a decrease in prices for the puppies from those other self-proclaimed registries.

But consumers deserve to know if they're dealing with a registry with 45,000 dogs in their LMX database, run by the breed founder, or one with thirty dogs in their database, run by a person that just prints certificates off from their home PC. If I were a consumer looking for a high-quality, properly-registered animal, I'd certainly want to know.

But if I had a fake registry, I wouldn't want people to know! The documentary would have brought the full Shiloh story into the public eye, and all of the fake Shiloh breeders would have been caught in an embarrassing position. It would have been financially detrimental to them, so they had no choice but to try to discredit me, in order to stop me from exposing the truth.

They didn't hesitate to resort to terribly dirty tricks.

More Problems

All hope for the documentary died. And then someone from one of the Shiloh splinter groups reported me to the department of agriculture. New laws had just been passed stating that New York State licensing was necessary if you produced more than twenty-five puppies a year. This was a law to control puppy mills. So the state came in and investigated me at New Zion. I wasn't worried.

I should have been.

My kennels were clean, and practically new—I thought they were perfect. But under new regulations, everything had to be nonporous. We had to tile and grout over all our concrete. Air purification systems had to be installed everywhere; wooden rails on the whelping boxes had to be removed because they were of porous material. Puppies couldn't run on grass, because that was a porous surface, so we had to make specially-sealed, epoxy-painted concrete surfaces for the puppies. It cost us almost forty thousand dollars, and it took us a year.

A lot of people rallied to our support again. Dawn Swick of Belle-Grace Kennels in Pennsylvania picked up some of our girls so that they could whelp at her home while all of the remodeling chaos was going on. Nancy Schmidt's husband Joe came down from New Jersey, driving eleven hours to my house on weekends to lay tile. Lisa learned to grout. Between people helping out, and donations that came in, we got the job done. But it was another heavy burden to overcome.

I tried to keep my head above water, to concentrate on all the good people I knew, and to think only about moving the dogs forward. But it was hard.

Left: large runs, April 2000.

Above: after renovations.

I attended the Cherry Blossom Classic again. A few of the old timers who had left in the club split were there and were very nice to me; they even asked me how I was doing. We talked a little bit. But there were also a few representatives of splinter factions who were disdainful of me.

Someone from another breed who was at the show asked me, "Why on earth do these people hate you so much? Didn't you create these dogs to begin with?"

I didn't know how to answer her.

At the show I had the opportunity to talk to a woman who had formerly been a good friend of mine, but who had left in the split. I decided to ask her directly: "Why do people hate me?"

She looked uncomfortable. Then she said, "Other people have a better vision for the breed than you do. You're too emotional, you look at things with tunnel vision, you don't look at the broad picture. I really think that these dogs could make a lot of money, but you're not interested in money. You just want to do the development thing." Then she walked away.

In other words, her vision and my vision for the future of the Shiloh Shepherd were different. Her vision included becoming a millionaire, and my vision was to produce the most awesome dog on earth.

I guess after all this time, people still think there is easy money that they're being prevented from making on Shiloh Shepherds because I'm in their way. But my response is the same as it always has been. If the quality isn't maintained, nobody will have anything to sell. There will be no customers—none at all. It won't matter who's sitting on top of the mountain if the whole thing comes crashing down!

When your goals are based on greed and your heart is in the wrong place, things just won't go right in the end. The "new" club lasted about three years. Then it broke up into four splinters: the SSBA, the NSBR, the USSDCR, and TSSR. I have seen some of their dogs in various shows, and with very few exceptions I have been unimpressed.

But something I learned a long time ago was that the only thing two breeders can agree upon is that the other one is wrong. Maybe those breeders think their dogs are doing great. As far as I'm concerned, they are welcome to do whatever they want to do, pursue millions of dollars, make whatever choices they want to make with their dogs.

But to call their dogs "Shiloh Shepherds" is unfair to what I have spent a lifetime trying to achieve.

As I left the Cherry Blossom Classic that year, my head was hanging as low as those of some of the dogs that were eliminated in the first round. I headed out to my car, and as I walked I said my own personal breeder's prayer: "God, please grant me the serenity to understand the things I cannot change; The wisdom I will need to produce only the best dogs possible. And the courage to do the right thing, no matter what people think."

The Last Battle—UKC Recognition

I have spies everywhere, including on "the dark side," as I sometimes call the splinter factions. In April of 2004, I got wind of something happening. Something big.

The various Shiloh Shepherd splinter factions were secretly planning to unite themselves. Lots of different names, each with their own initials indicating that they register Shiloh Shepherds.

The groups got together and said, Tina's exposing us on the Internet. Let's all unite under one umbrella under a real, legitimate organization. Then we can take all of our little databases and unite them, offer free club membership, and then we'll see if the UKC will accept us as the official Shiloh Shepherd club.

It was quite an underhanded plan.

If the UKC recognized the Shiloh Shepherd, and the splinter groups were the ones who had registered it, they would have the name, and it would be protected under the UKC. They would get legitimacy, and Tina Barber would be out in the cold; the name "Shiloh Shepherd" would officially belong to them.

The plan would never have worked if they had applied to the FIC, or FAC, or any of those fake registries. Everybody knows that they're phonies. Those registries are like colleges that advertise on the Internet and say, send us a hundred bucks, and we'll send you an MBA. But the UKC is the United Kennel Club, it has a long-time reputation. Traditionally it was for hunting and sporting dogs; it was never really an all-breed registry like the AKC. But the UKC had recently been purchased by a man named Wayne Cavanaugh, who opened the doors to all the breeds. When he announced that he was accepting rare breeds, the splinter groups went for it.

Why didn't I apply myself? If anybody should get recognition for the Shiloh Shepherd name, it should be the founder of Shiloh Kennels!

Because the breed is not finished, and it would be foolhardy to seek recognition until it is. If the stud books were closed now, the Shiloh would self-destruct before the end of this decade!

The splinter factions, however, didn't see any reason to wait. They wanted to take a breed based on my dogs but which they had developed in ways I would not have chosen, and register it under my kennel name.

As soon as I got wind of their plan, I must admit I went ballistic. Within three weeks from the time I found out about it, I raised holy hell. It was not my most Christian moment.

I worked nonstop eighteen-hour days to stop the UKC from recognizing the splinter factions. I've been in this business for forty years, and I have friends everywhere. I contacted the Coton de Tulear people, the White Shepherd people, and many other rare breed groups. Even the wolf dog folks were outraged. A few of my friends in the German Shepherd community were very strong in their support for me. They went after the UKC with both barrels blasting, saying "How dare you even consider such a thing, are you people out of your mind?"

Everyone could see that there was a difference between recognizing a rare breed, and recognizing a collection of splinters claiming to represent that breed. Mr. Cavanaugh was attacked from every corner of the world. Not just by little old Tina, but by armies of dog people. I called in every favor I had.

More importantly, the outcry was heard from coast to coast among our own Shiloh Shepherd membership. As soon as people knew what was happening, letters of support for the ISSR started pouring in. One of our members suggested that we all sign a petition and send it to the UKC president.

The petition got 138 signatures in less than three days. Over one hundred letters of protest were also sent to Mr. Cavanaugh by Shiloh Shepherd owners. These letters, written from the heart, moved me deeply. Once again, I remembered the power of all the good people who had never abandoned me.

God was with me all the way through it, and in the end, the battle didn't last long. Mr. Cavanaugh said, "No way will I even consider these people's request for recognition," and he dumped the whole thing.

We had triumphed.

I am writing this letter to express my feelings about the UKC possibly accepting the "Shiloh Shepherd" into their registry. I am absolutely against this being allowed to happen, and I completely support Tina Barber and her decades of work developing this breed.

The group that is attempting to get their so-called Shiloh Shepherds into the UKC is being led by a small group of people that are former members of our club. They left, or were asked to leave, because they did not want to work within our club and registry rules or work under the direction of the breed founder, who has set the ultimate path for the development of her breed.

These dissident breeders have started numerous registries over the years to attempt to compete with the ISSR, only to see each of them crash and then be reorganized under new names as their internal alliances have shifted. They have not been able to band together or work together long enough to gain the recognition they desire because they haven't been able to stop the fighting amongst their ever-shifting factions.

Due to the number of times that these people have split and shifted alliances among themselves, I would be critical of the accuracy of their record-keeping and wary of the trustworthiness of the documentation on their dogs. After all, all of these breeders (after leaving the ISSR) have been printing their registration papers off on home computers in their own home-based registries... what better way to fake data and mess with pedigrees? At each fight and subsequent split, data has surely been lost and has had to be creatively "recreated" to make it look acceptable enough for them to attempt to buffalo their way into the UKC.

As all of this bickering and fighting has been going on between these rogue breeders, they lost what credibility they may once have had in the dog world. Many have had difficulty selling their puppies and their quest for UKC recognition is strictly for their own monetary gain, not for the good of the breed. They desire to get their dogs into the UKC because they feel that it will give them much-needed coordination and the credibility that they sorely lack. They feel that UKC recognition will finally give ability to sell their dogs to the unknowing public with "real" registration papers. Many of the puppies that they currently are registering as Shiloh Shepherds are nothing more than German Shepherd mixes. Due to their extremely small gene pool and unknowledgeable breeding choices, they have had to heavily resort to numerous "crosses" to attempt to correct severe health and temperament issues. All of this tampering with their "version" of the breed has taken it further and further from the true path that Tina Barber has set for the original ISSR Shilohs.

Please be assured that the many thousands of ISSR supporters are right now being organized to publicly fight for the integrity of our breed. We are furious over the proposed induction of the splinter breeders' dogs into the UKC and will do everything possible to publicize the atrocity that is being perpetuated against Tina Barber and the breed that she is still developing.

Is the paltry sum of money that would be raised by registering this small group of dogs worth sullying the UKC's reputation? We ask you to deny admittance of these rogues and their mixed breed dogs to the UKC.

Debbie Knatz
SSDCA Advisory Board Member
Genetic Task Force Member
Shepherd's Ridge

To Whom it May Concern,

I have been involved with the Shiloh Shepherds since 1994 and watched the breed go through many changes. I believe that the only registry dedicated to preserving the vision of the breed is the International Shiloh Shepherd Registry (ISSR). All other registries are splinters of the original with insufficient dogs (hence data) to back up their breeding programs and the future health and well being of the Shiloh Shepherd. I am strongly opposed to any registry applying for new breed application with the UKC other than the ISSR.

At such time when the registry feels that the breed is established, then we may apply for recognition. Until then, accept no substitutes.

We hope that you see our point and do not allow the recognition of Shiloh Shepherds at this time. Thank you.

Sincerely,

Pamela Moody

Highlife Kennels

October 18, 2004
Mr. Wayne A. Cavanaugh
United Kennel Club
100 East Kilgore Rd
Kalamazoo, MI 49002-5584

Subject: Breed Recognition

Dear Mr. Cavanaugh,

As you may already know, a splinter group has asked your organization for breed recognition as original Shiloh Shepherds.

My husband and I have been longstanding members of the Shiloh Shepherd Dog Club of America, Inc. and have supported our International Shiloh Shepherd Registry since 1992. I have served on the Advisory Board for 5 years and am now serving for one year. I also collect data for our health survey program for healthier Shilohs.

We have had three Shilohs, one of which is deceased. These Shilohs are so magnificent that these splinter groups want to go on their greedy way to make money and do not care about their puppy buyers or their dogs. They are hoping your United Kennel Club will recognize them. Please investigate them before they ruin your United Kennel Club's good name.

Sincerely,
Pat and Dale Urso

To Whom It May Concern,

It has come to our attention that a group of people who left the ISSR (International Shiloh Shepherd Registry) have banded together and petitioned the UKC for breed recognition with your organization.

I am writing this letter in hopes of helping to sway your votes to "no" on this issue. The Shiloh Shepherd IS still a breed being developed.

The only person who has the key to locking the stud book closed is Tina Barber and those breeders who continue to breed under her guidance. The only person who should have the right to apply to the UKC (or any other registry) is Tina Barber.

The ISSR and the SSDCA (Shiloh Shepherd Club of America) are THE ONLY Registry and Dog Club which have stood the test of time within the Shiloh Shepherd community. All other registries and clubs (including those who have applied with the UKC) have risen and fallen so often that no one can even keep straight who they are and who they represent.

I think it would be an absolute travesty for all present and future Shiloh Shepherd owners if you were to accept an unfinished breed into the UKC at this time. Please read carefully and follow all the links of the e-mail letter sent from our club secretary.

Thank you for taking the time to read and listen to those of us who stand with the ISSR and the SSDCA.

Pam Dymond-Weed
owned by three
Shiloh Shepherds
and SSDCA Advisory
Board Member

To: Wayne Cavanaugh
United Kennel Club
100 East Kilgore Rd.
Kalamazoo, MI 49002-5584

Dear Mr. Cavanaugh,

It is my understanding that you have been sent an Application for Breed Recognition of the Shiloh Shepherd. This application comes to you from a few "disheartened" breeders. I am aware that the ISSR and the SSDCA have sent you a "letter of disgust" in this matter. Rightly so. I am appalled that an organization such as the United Kennel Club, respected for many, many years, is even entertaining the idea.

This club that has petitioned you for recognition does not have the necessary gene pool to properly develop this breed. They also do not have the LMX data, or access to the relationship coefficient numbers. That is correct, Mr Cavanaugh: the Shiloh Shepherd is a breed still under development. To give access and recognition of this "fragile breed" to these "dissidents" at this time would be to destroy the Shiloh Shepherd. I assure you, Mr Cavanaugh, we will not let that happen.

Be very careful, Mr. Cavanaugh. These other dogs that they are trying to pass off as Shiloh Shepherds ARE NOT!!! They are an uncontrolled mixture of many, many dogs.

I am a Member In Good Standing with the SSDCA. My wife and I are enrolled in the breed founder's Official Shiloh Shepherd Academy, where we will become licensed breeders within the ISSR. Currently, we own one Shiloh Shepherd. Her name is Serenity Hills Golden Orca of Zion, aka "Orca." I have included a picture of her with my children. We are a licensed business within the Commonwealth of Kentucky, listed as Serenity Hill Shilohs.

We will be purchasing another breeding female this fall from a licensed breeder with the ISSR. Next year we intend to purchase two more breeding females, again ONLY from a licensed ISSR breeder. When we begin our breeding program in the fall of 2005, we will ONLY register our litters with the ISSR. Our current plans are to have two litters a year starting in the year 2005. All will ONLY be registered with the ISSR.

I painstakingly researched this breed for two years. I talked with several breeders, not all with the ISSR. After my exhaustive research, I found the ISSR and the SSDCA to be the ONLY registries. Their professionalism was unmatched. Their knowledge was unsurpassed. Their Shiloh Shepherds are unequalled.

Also, it is clear to everyone that Tina Barber is the ONLY recognized breed founder of these magnificent dogs, the Shiloh Shepherds. That was one main reason I purchased from an ISSR breeder. Even on the other kennel websites, many also recognize Tina Barber as the breed founder of the original Shiloh Shepherd. By name.

So, we must ask ourselves, Why? Why did some leave the ISSR and the SSDCA? And then try and steal the Shiloh Shepherd name and gain recognition with the UKC?

The answer, Mr. Cavanaugh, is simple: GREED!!! The kennel clubs are supposed to have the best interest of the dogs in mind. That was the vision of the United Kennel Club's founders, many years ago.

I am sure, after careful thought and consideration, you will DENY this request of theirs. As an owner and avid dog lover, I ask that you read all the evidence being presented to you. I then must ask you to DENY this request.

Thank you very much for taking the time to read this.

Sincerely,
Yvette and Willie Lass
Serenity Hill Shilohs
Flatwoods, KY

To the UKC:

I've been advised that you are considering registering dogs that have been purported to you to be "Shiloh Shepherds."

I know a little something about AUTHENTIC Shiloh Shepherds, having traveled to Gainesville, NY, USA in 1991 and having personally purchased one from the breed founder, Tina Barber, following about five years of personal investigation into GSD's and similar dogs.

The dog I obtained from her was truly exceptional and a testament to her lifelong work; he was the smartest, handsomest, most trainable and most impressive dog I have ever owned. Even so, Tina Barber is still working to further perfect the Shiloh Shepherd breed, and the credit for the development of this breed (and for the NAME, "SHILOH SHEPHERD") belongs to her, and her alone.

Please be advised that if you are not dealing with Tina Barber and her licensed breeders and the International Shiloh Shepherd Registry (ISSR) you will NOT be dealing with AUTHENTIC and GENUINE Shiloh Shepherds, and the inevitable result will be that the Shiloh Shepherd breed will suffer; purchasers of dogs which are purported to be Shiloh Shepherds, but which are not ISSR-registered dogs, will not be getting the quality they came to expect and will ultimately be unhappy; and the reputation and credibility of your own organization will ultimately suffer.

I urge you to investigate carefully and to view purported Shiloh Shepherds with skepticism. You will find that what I am telling you is true. Do not allow upstarts, renegades and poseurs to trade on and profit from the reputation that Tina Barber has worked all her life for.

Please feel free to contact me should you require additional information or wish to discuss this further. Thank you.

Cheers,

Stu Tarlowe

Rosedale, Kansas, USA

Shiloh Shepherd and GSD fancier and Life Member, Shiloh Shepherd Dog Club of America

I know that one of the things God wants me to do is stop freaking out over stuff. But I am also beginning to understand my limitations—I can't stop freaking, much as I'd like to. That's me. God keeps putting these tests before me, and I take them, and then I have to take them again. Some of the people in my life who have always made me mad continue to pop up and make my blood boil.

Forgiveness is something that has never come easily to me. I do work at it, though.

But I also believe that there are times when God wants me to fight. The heroes of the Bible have all been fighters, in one way or another, especially in the Old Testament. I'm a good fighter, and I fight for things that I believe in. That's a part of me, too.

I learned to let God take control in those days after the fire, when that was my only option. But now that I can have control again, it's still my tendency to seize it. That's why God has to show me repeatedly: if things are not going my way, instead of beating my head against a wall trying to regain control, I should just let Him take over, and doors will open. The UKC battle is just another perfect example of His power. Just like the verse that the Lord gave me in '97 when I knew that the "new" club was going to "take over" after Homecoming. I had my NESSA chapter rehearse their drill team performance that year to the tune of these verses. As the splinters sat there waiting for the show to begin, the music started—and the Shilohs walked in to *"I have given you authority to tread on snakes and scorpions, and over all the power of the enemy: and nothing shall by any means hurt you."* Luke 10:19.

I learn, and I learn, and I learn again.

Chapter 9

Final Steps

Triumph

The Shiloh Shepherd has documentation like no other breed. Other breeds have pedigrees that tell you a bunch of names; our pedigree tells you how tall the dog was, how much he weighed as an adult, what color he was, what kind of temperament he had, what kind of coat he had, what his littermates looked like, his health data, genetic data... We have a registry that is more complex and more detailed than any other dog registry in the world.

Even more importantly, nearly forty years of highly selective breeding has produced an amazing dog. Just as their ancestors herded and protected their sheep, the Shilohs love and protect their family members, especially the children. They are highly intelligent animals, and possess no limitations in their ability to perform as search and rescue dogs, in herding, as STM competition dogs, or as therapy dogs. They excel in any and all obedience competitions, and love to strut their stuff at dog shows!

Real Shiloh Shepherds get very big. It's not unusual for some males to reach up to 32" at the withers. Most average 30", which is still closer to the standard of a Saint Bernard, or even a small Great Dane, than to a normal German Shepherd. The Shiloh Shepherds of the twenty-first century have the strength and reliability of the old-time German Shepherds, with the fine-tuned intelligence, friendliness and beauty that comes only from extremely careful breeding.

But the breed is still not finished. Not yet.

Adam and Josh, Homecoming 2003.

Meg and Josh at the NCA show 2005.

New Zion Shilohs

Hypothetically it takes only four generations of breeding "type" to establish a new strain of dogs. So why is the Shiloh Shepherd still under development?

Our "under development" status won't change until a solid gene pool base of unrelated dogs has been established, and that process takes a long time. In our case, hundreds of litters have been born, thousands of puppies have been tested, and *only* the best possible offspring have been used in breeding. Development has taken a long time because our goal is an unquestionably superior dog. My aim has never been for the Shiloh Shepherd dogs to be "good enough" to gain recognition as a breed; perfection, as close to it as possible, is my personal goal. Recognition will be a happy reward.

We've come a long way. From developing the three foundation dogs in the 1970s to our first outcrosses, Samson and Sabrina, things were right on track. Our gene pool got chopped up in the switch to the AKC, which couldn't be helped. Then, just as we were about to expand the gene pool sufficiently for full recognition, we had the "back issue" hysteria and the club split, and then the splinter attacks that followed. Those slowed things down a lot. Of course, even in the worst of times we always had a solid base of great dogs, so we were hardly starting from scratch. But getting a lot of diversity takes time, especially if people leave. Finally, and most unexpectedly of all, the fire reduced my stock dramatically, and we were forced to regroup yet again.

At last, now we are ready to move forward and complete the breed.

My personal breeding situation has changed, as I now have trustworthy licensed breeders, and I rely on them to help. We're down to about thirty-eight dogs on the New Zion property. I have stepped back in terms of day-to-day work; my daughter Lisa is taking over many of the hands-on jobs that I used to do. She supervises the feedings, the wormings, and some of the grooming, and I have a crew that comes in two or three times a week to deal with the extra heavy duty cleaning of the kennels. My son John also helps out, as he always has, and Lisa's husband Jamie still comes and goes like always. We have a pretty small crew, so we all stay very busy. As breed warden, I am still in control of the direction of the breed, from general genetic counseling to specific breeding decisions. But it is nice to be able to hand most of the physical work over to my licensed breeders and to my daughter.

> Since 1974, Shiloh Shepherd owners and fanciers from across the continent (and beyond) have had the privilege of attending a yearly Homecoming, an event started by our breed founder, Tina Barber, and sponsored, since 1991, by the Shiloh Shepherd Dog Club of America, Inc.
>
> From humble beginnings in 1974, these weekends have turned into an informal yearly family reunion for dogs and their owners, with four days of seminars and shows, time to make new friends and renew old friendships, but most importantly they provide Tina and all of the future breeders an opportunity to evaluate the progeny they have been producing over the years. Shilohs and their owners come from all corners of the U.S. and Canada and even overseas to participate in the various activities. Despite moves, divorces, and even tragedies, the Homecoming event has never failed to occur for all Shiloh owners to enjoy. Many even plan their family vacation a year in advance in order not to miss this annual event.

Homecoming is still going strong. I'm bossing everybody around as usual—it feels like old times. However, Lisa has actively taken over most of the organization's responsibilities. It's a lot of work, but she has been doing a great job! Every year we have more and more Shiloh lovers coming to Upstate New York for the festivities. Recently at Homecoming we were proud to announce the formation of the SSC (Swiss Shiloh Chapter), headed up by Gabriele Wellik of Switzerland in co-operation with our own SSDCA, Inc. and the ISSR. We are now, officially, an internationally-celebrated breed.

Back at home, I keep pretty busy. I still mail out Shiloh tracts for each inquiry, just as I have done since 1974, which allows the dogs to reach people directly. I also spend a lot of time writing articles for our Shiloh Shepherd website (www.shilohshepherd.com) and the Shiloh Shepherd Learning Center (http://ShilohShepherds.info), teaching the public about the breed. Presently we have scores of articles up on our websites, and this number will continue to increase on a regular basis.

Our Shiloh Shepherds Community Forums (http://shilohshepherds.infopop.cc/groupee) began with a small group of members in 1999 and have been growing steadily since. We now have nearly a thousand regular members, and we expect that to expand to several thousand by the end of this decade. The forums help me to keep my finger on the pulse of the breed: I get constant updates on what people are thinking, and how both dogs and people interrelate. On the bulletin boards I work with owners on a personal basis, telling them how to raise their dogs properly.

Everybody has always called me "Ma Shiloh." I actually enjoy this nickname, especially when people who are celebrities in their own right call me "Ma." It's very endearing to me. Once the puppies go to new homes, I keep on mothering those dogs, and their owners, with the help of the Internet. You just don't send your kids off when they turn eighteen and say goodbye! I keep counseling them, making sure that the dogs and the people are all okay. I'm like the Dear Abby of the Shiloh Shepherd community.

***

After all this time, and all my losses, I truly understand the value of good people to this breed. I especially appreciate my licensed breeders. After the fire, many wonderful people came into the breeding program. Those are the breeders who I hope will continue to help me take the Shiloh Shepherd to its completion. Creating a breed takes a lot of people, logistically speaking. In order to truly understand our gene pool, we need progeny from each possible combination. That's a lot of dogs!

I tell my breeders it's like digging for gold. We've got a hundred-acre plot, and if we have enough people each looking through a small square, we'll eventually find what we're looking for. Whereas, if we have only me and Lisa out there with a shovel, there's a good chance we'll never find it. It's a numbers game.

I've revised my Very Important Breeder program to fit the new mindset of the licensed Shiloh breeders that will carry this breed forth in the new millennium. The requirements are much stricter now than they were fifteen years ago, and they keep getting stricter all the time. I lost so much gene pool to unscrupulous breeders that it's much harder for me to do this just on trust: If breeders don't follow the format, they're out. I got a lot tougher once I realized how easily money could corrupt people.

In exchange for my breeders' help, support, and dedication, I provide honest representation, follow up, counseling (including spiritual) and friendship to all. It has not escaped my notice that one of the things any association must be good for—even a dog association—is to care for its people.

Over the years I have received a lot of love and care from my Shiloh Shepherd breeders and fanciers. It is my intention to give it back whenever it's needed.

Two-year-old Konrad Braveheart of Zion.

Final Steps

In 2004 the Shiloh Shepherd officially turned thirty, and I turned fifty-seven. I've done plenty, and I've learned plenty. I finally have a good handle on where we are, and what we need to do.

The breed is ready for completion.

Orbit and Artus were good outcross lines from the late 1990s, but it is already time for new blood again. In 2005, I selected our final three outcrosses. Those dogs are already entered into our database, and we're breeding them in Europe right now. Lisa will also be going to Europe to select puppies and bring them back here. Then I'll selectively place them with people I trust, as we breed them back into our gene pool.

After that, we've made a decision to be drastic: we're going to have a massive gene pool expansion in the next three years. Our three new outcrosses will help us get over this hump so that we can inbreed, and at that point the breed can solidify and become genetically diverse enough to be recognized. I'm hoping to close the studbooks by 2009—that would add up to thirty-five years of trials and triumphs that I walked through with my Savior.

Now that I can see the Lord's plan, it makes it much easier to press forth towards the finish line. The Shiloh Shepherd is almost done.

The FCI, or The Fédération Cynologique Internationale, also called the World Canine Organization, is the most prestigious dog registry in the world. It is known for being extremely strict about registering dogs. We are applying for FCI certification for the Shiloh Shepherd, which will allow us to show our dogs internationally—Mexico, Europe, Asia. The Shiloh Shepherd will be recognized everywhere.

But the FCI has never recognized an American "rare" breed before. The FCI recognizes only the AKC in the United States, and the CKC in Canada, so unless you belong to one of those organizations, you can't get legitimate recognition. What we are planning to do is to go beyond the normal parameters and reach out to the foremost dog organization in the world. This has not surprised any of the people that truly know me, because they have always seen me reach for "the unreachable star," and often catch it!

We've already applied for recognition of the Shiloh Shepherd from SKG, or Schweizerische Kynologische Gesellschaft, the all-breed kennel club of Switzerland. Once we have FCI recognition, we can walk into the AKC and get into the miscellaneous class, because we will finally be a real breed.

My Biggest Regret

I can't help but feel sad about all the dogs that could have been Shiloh Shepherds had their owners not pulled them out of the ISSR database. It's an unhappy fact that mass-produced, unpapered "Shilohs" are still worth a lot of money—the name "Shiloh," even when used inappropriately, still goes a long way! Money often motivates people to make bad decisions. The breed has suffered for it.

Inferior-quality puppies calling themselves "Shiloh" are all over the market. It is such a shame. I continue to feel sorry for all of the people who have been deceived into purchasing GSD-mixed pups that were fraudulently represented as Shiloh Shepherds. If those unscrupulous breeders had attempted to represent themselves as "Tina M. Barber" they could be arrested for identity theft, but unfortunately a "breed" of dog does not carry that kind of protection, unless it is fully recognized. At this point we are still "under development" and will continue to stay here, until we cross over the finish line that I have been struggling towards for all these years.

I can't help thinking about those old dogs that should have had a chance to properly contribute their genes to this breed. Instead, their names will never be able to appear on the roster that will go down in the history books. Just like all the names of the original GSD's that first contributed to the expansion of that breed, I honestly believe that the dogs that are still within the ISSR today, and producing puppies, will soon have their chance to shine too. What a day of rejoicing that will be!

However, I am thankful for the Internet. It has given me an opportunity to share the true history of these dogs, and to make real and meaningful connections with current and future Shiloh owners.

The day will come when this insanity is exposed, and people will take more time to investigate the truth behind these so-called "rare" breeds before spending thousands of dollars for genetically inferior imposters.

As for the backyard breeders, well, their money train will have been derailed by the truth!

Lisa Barber—Heir Apparent

A lot of people don't think of Lisa as an authority because she's my child. It's understandable, I suppose. People might think, "Well, yeah, that's just her kid. What does she know?"

Lisa knows a lot. She's been running dogs through their routines since she was seven years old. Lisa is quite a bit like me: She got in trouble for skipping school, getting into fights—she just wanted to be out riding horses or training dogs. She's an excellent trainer, with an innate understanding of animals, and no fear. She belongs in the world of dog breeding.

Lisa is amazing at spotting dogs. She excels at evaluating structure—her "eye" is right on. She can do relationship coefficients and all the other complicated computer work for the Shiloh Shepherd. Sometimes I have a tendency to have what we call "Oldtimers"—not Alzheimers!—when I'm going through pedigrees. Occasionally I'll skip a generation, and she'll say, "Oh, you missed that one." She's right on top of things.

So it is a special satisfaction for me to pass my work on to the next generation, especially since I have always thought of myself as carrying on my grandmother's work. There's no way the Shiloh could finish running the race without Lisa ready to grab the reins at a moment's notice.

There's still a lot of work to be done.

Training.

Tina, Lisa and her three sons at the 2003 Homecoming.

Full Circle

The Shiloh is so full of potential it's amazing. Even so, it has been ten years since we had a ring full of dogs of the caliber of the 1995 Cherry Blossom Classic, the show that brought me so much joy. Splinter wars have driven a lot of great dog owners and even breeders into hiding.

In my low moments, sometimes I wondered if I would ever feel like things were on the right track again. The new millennium started off horribly for me, with the fire, the documentary disaster, and the struggle to remake our kennels to code. Then, when I was already feeling worn down, the UKC fiasco sapped the last of my energy. I had reached my lowest point.

And that's when I saw the Lord's blessing once again. I think He does these things to keep me encouraged!

We did a breeding down in Pennsylvania on a co-ownership. Lisa came back with the puppies that she had selected, and she walked up the stairs with one of them in her arms. I have a painting on our wall that a friend of Lisa's gave me of Shep and Laz, two of my all-time favorite dogs. Lisa was holding this puppy, standing in front of the picture. She said, "What do you think, Mom?"

I thought that she was being weird, and I asked her to come closer to the couch so I could see the puppy. She refused, and insisted that I just walk over to the wall and look at him. What was I supposed to be looking for? If she wanted an evaluation, she needed to set him up on the coffee table, not hold him in front of the painting.

Shep painting.   *Remembering Shep through Smokey.*

Then I looked, and I looked again... I've seen literally thousands of pups, but that face! I looked at the picture, and then back at Smokey, the pup. The markings were identical. This puppy looked just like our Shep!

Lisa said, "Did I guess right? He's going to grow up to look like Shep?" I said, "Set him down," so she set him down, she moved him, and I couldn't believe it. It was like the clock had turned back sixteen years.

I said, "Exactly. Identical. This dog is going to grow up to be a carbon-copy of Shep." I had to blink back some tears in my eyes.

I stood up to examine him closer. I asked her to let him run around the room, and within minutes he stopped in front of the fireplace and walked into a perfect stack. He was a miniature version of Shep, in every detail. This could not be happening!

I went full force into my cutthroat inspection, looking for faults, but I could not find any. I haven't seen a pup like that for many years.

The breeding was Lisa's idea. She was trying to recreate a dog like Shep, and she did it. That's a big deal for a breeder, because to "recreate" a dog is almost impossible. Lisa was young when Bionic Black Smoke, her Shep, was born, and he was one of the first dogs she showed, at age fourteen. She'll be showing this puppy, Smokey, next month in Canada.

Smokey gave me an extremely well-timed boost, one that I desperately needed. I could not have been more thrilled.

Or could I?

GV Ch Bionic Black Smoke of Zion ROM.

Two weeks later I was invited to visit one of my licensed breeders and take a look at a litter of three-week-old pups. It was still very early in the game, and I was just taking a "sneak preview," with no expectations at all.

Those puppies were huge! They had huge bone, and nice heads... The biggest one looked like he would be plush, which was good. But there was something else that was tugging at me. Weird. What was it? I saw the two males next to each other and had a déjà vu. Had I seen those two pups before? Where? When?

Then I recalled Bullet and Kodiak, two dogs from the '90s. They were the only two Yetti had in that litter, and the giant plush coat was later lost during the splinter wars. Bullet became a casualty of the fire; we had to foster him out and he was unfortunately killed in a car accident. Was I about to get a second chance? Would Danny turn into a giant that would someday leave his mark on the Shiloh Shepherd gene pool?

Danny and Smokey met at my house several weeks later, and just being able to watch them play gave me an incredible emotional high. We were coming full circle: the dogs of the future looked like the ones from my past! I had not dared to dream that after all we've been through, dogs like these would be a reality in 2004. They are miracles, like the ones I began seeing back in the late '70s, when things finally began to work. All my mistakes, all my heartaches, all my tragedies, all the people who tried to hurt me... When I saw those puppies, I forgot them all.

It has all been worth it.

Smokey and Danny.

On our Shiloh bulletin board, Willie Lass, one of my licensed breeders, asked if his kids would still be able to find a real Shiloh Shepherd twenty years from now. Now I can honestly answer him, "Yes! Yes! Yes!" I know these dogs are going to be more than okay—they are going to be as amazing as they ever were!

Back to The Future

I became a breeder because I had a dog that I was madly in love with, and I wanted to "recreate" that dog, so that other people could have the pleasure of owning one like him. So I kept working at it, and working at it, and learning, and studying, and working some more. For me, I still think of Rex, the dog I had as a child. But I've come across great dogs that I've been crazy about since then, like Luke, and Laz, and many other ones. At this point it's not just one particular dog in my mind. It's a group of dogs, both plush and smooth, both male and female. Those dogs are strong, and big, and powerful, but gentle, smart and loving.

Those dogs are known as the Shiloh Shepherd.

Like many people, I want to leave behind a legacy. Some people leave behind something that is beneficial to humanity, and I would like to think I'm one of them. Every dog lover should own a Shiloh Shepherd, and I hope that one day there will be enough Shiloh Shepherd dogs for every person who wants one. Those dogs are my legacy to the world.

As for myself personally, I know that I have not fought my last battle. For everything that goes right on this path of mine, there is always something that goes wrong.

I'm prepared.

Shiloh Shepherds have developed slowly, the gene pool has stabilized, and the club and the registry have transformed themselves into strong associations of good people. I have been changing too. Slowly, and with difficulty, I have been learning to let God take control.

Many years ago, a Hebrew friend who had been attending Rabbinical classes in Israel told me that the literal Hebrew translation of "Shiloh" is "Rest in the Lord." Rest in the Lord: be at peace, and let Him do the work, and that's when you'll see miracles happening. Shiloh—rest in the Lord—is what I have learned for myself.

And Shiloh is what I offer to all whom I meet in person, or who read about me, and a dog straight from the heart of God.

The Shiloh Shepherd Illustrated Breed Standard
As written by

Tina M. Barber
Shiloh Shepherd™ Breed Founder
Illustrations by Linda Shaw, MBA

1) GENERAL APPEARANCE: The Shiloh Shepherd™ portrays a distinct impression of nobility with a unique aura of intelligence, that radiates a sense of regal wisdom and strength. Powerfully built with unsurpassed beauty and elegance; a picture of true balance; each part being in harmonious proportion to every other part, and to the whole. Being of giant size does not deter from his proud carriage or seemingly effortless movement. His total devotion and willingness to work can be seen in his alert eyes, and his happy attitude. Timidity, frailty, sullenness, viciousness, and lack of animation, impair the general character of this breed. A certain amount of aloofness is acceptable as long as it is not associated with any form of sharp-shyness.

2) CHARACTER: Courageous and self-confident, this gentle giant possesses superior intelligence wrapped in a heart of gold, faithfully protecting his home and those he loves. This extremely versatile and easily trained companion loves to swim, carry packs for the mountain climber, endure long trail rides, or pull heavy sleds. His excellent Air Scenting ability can be utilized in various ways.

    As a true, loyal Flock Guardian descendant, he is steady and bold without undue aggression; ready to die fighting for those in his care; yet sweet and loving when playing with small children, animals, or comforting the elderly.

3) HEAD: The head is broad and noble, slightly domed and in proportion to the body. The width and length of the skull are approximately equal with a gently defined stop, strong developed cheekbones, and a gradually tapering muzzle. The muzzle should be predominantly black, the length being equal to that of the forehead, with the lips firmly fitted and solid black. The muzzle should not be long, narrow, or snipey in appearance.

4) EARS: Ears are moderately pointed in proportion to the skull, open toward the front and carried erect when at attention, well rounded, triangular in shape, well cupped, stiff, height equal to width at base. If ear is folded forward for measuring length, tip should not pass upper eye rim. Set high and well apart, the base of the ear is placed above the center of the eye. A mature dog with hanging ears must be disqualified.

5) EYES: Shades of dark to very light brown will be accepted (no other colors are allowed), of medium size, almond shaped, set a little obliquely and not protruding. The expression should be keen, intelligent, and composed.

6) TEETH: 42 in number (20 upper and 22 lower) strongly developed and meeting in a scissor bite in which part of the inner surface of upper incisor meets and engages part of the outer surface of the lower incisors. An overshot or undershot jaw is a DISQUALIFYING FAULT.

7) NECK: The neck is strong and muscular, relatively long and slightly arched. Proportionate in size to the head and without loose skin. When the dog is at attention with head raised and neck carried high a look of nobility should be easily observed.

8) FOREQUARTERS: The shoulder blades are long and obliquely angled, laid flat and not placed forward. The upper arm joins the shoulder blade at about a right angle. Both the upper arm and the shoulder blade are well muscled. The forelegs, viewed from the side, are straight but heavy boned and oval rather than round. The pasterns are strong and springy and angulated at approximately a 25 degree angle from the vertical.

9) FEET: The feet are oval, compact, with toes well arched, pads thick and firm, nails short and dark. Dew claws, if any should be removed from the hind legs. Dewclaws on the forelegs are left on. **Splay or hare feet should be considered a VERY SERIOUS FAULT.**

10) PROPORTION: The Shiloh Shepherd™ should appear longer than tall. The desired height for males, at the top the highest point of the shoulder blade, can be no less than 28" with the ideal height of 30" or more preferred. For females, the desired height can be no less than 26" with the ideal height of 28" or more preferred. The minimum weight for dogs should not be less than 120 pounds at maturity (three years), with the ideal being 140 to 160 pounds. Minimal weight for bitches is 80 pounds at maturity and the ideal being 100 to 120 pounds.

The length measured from the point of the prosternum or breastbone to the rear edge of the pelvis, the ischial tuberosity, with the

LINDA SHAW

most desirable proportion of 10 to 9. ANY MALE THAT MEASURES LESS THAN 28" OR FEMALES LESS THAN 26" AT MATURITY (36 MONTHS OF AGE) SHOULD BE DISQUALIFIED.

11) BODY: The entire body should appear to be well coordinated, yet muscular and solid. The back is broad and straight, strongly boned, and well developed. There should be good depth of brisket. A roach back should be considered a SERIOUS FAULT, as should a soft or sway back. The body should not appear spindly or extremely leggy. All proportions must be well balanced.

LINDA SHAW

12) CHEST: Commencing at the prosternum, it is well filled and carried well down between the legs. It is deep and capacious, never shallow, with ample room for lungs and heart, carried well forward, with the sternum showing ahead of the shoulder profile.

13) RIBS: Well sprung and long, neither barrel shaped nor too flat, and carried down to the sternum which reaches to the elbows. Correct ribbing allows the elbows to move freely when the dog is at a trot. Too round causes interference and throws the elbows out; too flat or short causes pinched elbows. Ribbing is carried well back so that the loin is relatively short.

14) ABDOMEN: Should be firmly held and not paunchy. The bottom line is only moderately tucked up in the loin.

15) TOPLINE: The withers are higher than and sloping into the lower back. The back is straight, very strongly developed without sag or roach and relatively short. The desirable long proportion is not derived from a long back but achieved by width of forequarter, length of withers, width of hindquarters, and position and length of croup viewed from the side. The loin, viewed from the top, is broad and strong (undue length between the last rib and thigh when viewed from the side is undesirable). The croup should be long and gradually sloping.

16) TAIL: Bushy with the last vertebra extending past the hock joint. It is set smoothly into the croup and should appear to hang as a plume. At rest the tail hangs in a slight curve like a saber. When the dog is excited or in motion, the curve is accentuated and the tail is raised, but it should never curl forward beyond the vertical line nor above the level of the back. The tail should never be carried straight out or rolled up over the back. A tail that is raised above the vertical line and/or past the horizontal line of the croup is a DISQUALIFYING FAULT. Tails that are too short, thin, or ratty should be severely penalized.

17) HINDQUARTERS: The whole assembly of the thigh, viewed from the side, is broad, with both upper and lower thigh well muscled, forming as nearly as possible a right angle. The upper thighbone parallels the shoulder blade while the lower thighbone parallels the upper arm. The metatarsus is short, strong, and tightly articulated.

18) GAIT: THE GAIT SHOULD BE CONSIDERED A VERY CRITICAL PART OF THE OVERALL PERFECTION OF THIS BREED. This breed must be observed while the dog is on a loose lead so that the natural gait is evident. The gait is outreaching, elastic, seemingly tireless without effort; smooth, and rhythmic, covering the maximum amount of ground with the minimum amount of steps. At a walk, it covers a great deal of ground with long strides of both hind legs and forelegs. At a trot, it covers still more ground with even longer stride, and moves powerfully but easily with coordination and balance, so that the gait appears to be as the steady motion of a well-lubricated machine.

The feet travel close to the ground on both forward reach and backward push. In order to achieve ideal movement of this kind, there must be good muscular development and ligamentation.

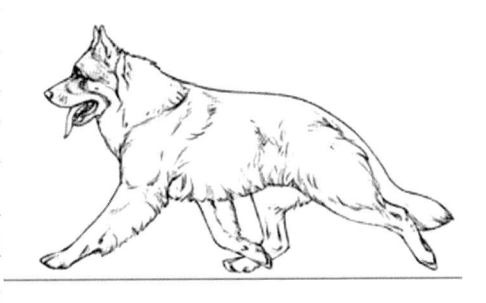

The hindquarters deliver, through the back, a powerful thrust, which slightly lifts the whole animal and drives the body forward. Reaching far under, and passing the imprint left by the front foot, the hind foot takes hold of the ground; then hock, stifle, and upper thigh come into play and sweep back, the stroke of the hind leg finishing with the foot still close to the ground in a smooth follow through. The overreach of the hindquarter usually necessitates one hind foot passing outside and the other hind foot passing inside the track of the forefeet, and such action is not faulty unless the locomotion is crab-wise with the dog's body sideways out of the normal straight line. As the dog increases speed into the "flying trot," he should move fluidly, without pounding. The forelegs should reach out well past the nose while the head is carried forward.

19) TRANSMISSION: The typical smooth, flowing gait is maintained with great strength and firmness of back. The whole effort of the hindquarter is transmitted to the forequarter through the loin, back, and withers. At full trot, the back must remain firm and level without sway, roll, whip, or roach. An uneven topline with withers lower than the croup is FAULTY. To compensate for the forward motion imparted by the hindquarters, the shoulder should open to its full extent. The forelegs should reach out close to the ground, in a long stride in harmony with that of the hindquarters. The dog does not track on widely separated paralleled lines, but brings the feet inward toward the middle line of the body when trotting, in order to maintain balance. The feet track closely but do not strike or cross over. Viewed from the front, the front legs function from the shoulder joint to the pad in a straight line. Viewed from the rear, the hind legs function from the hip joint to the pad in a straight line. FAULTS OF GAIT, WHETHER VIEWED FROM THE FRONT, REAR OR SIDE, ARE CONSIDERED VERY SERIOUS.

20) COLOR: The Shiloh Shepherd™ comes in various colors. Shades of black with tan, golden tan, reddish tan, silver, and cream are as desirable as are various shades of richly pigmented golden, silver, red, dark brown, dark gray, or black sables. Also solid black or solid white is acceptable as long as the nose, eye rims, and lips are solid black. A white blaze on the chest is acceptable as well as some white markings on the toes, as long as they are blended in with the other shades of silver, cream, tan, etc. Any other white markings on any other part of the body should be considered a FAULT. Any washed out or pale colors should also be considered a FAULT. Blues, livers, dogs with lack of proper pigmentation, or dogs with a nose that is not predominately black must be DISQUALIFIED.

21) COAT (TWO ACCEPTABLE VARIETIES): SMOOTH: The ideal dog has a double coat of medium length. The outer coat should be as dense as possible with hair straight, harsh, lying close to the body. The hair around the neck area should be slightly longer and thicker. The rear of the forelegs and hind legs has somewhat longer hair extending to the pastern and hock respectively. The head including the inner ear and fore face, legs and paws should be covered with shorter hair. Even though the smooth coated type requires less care and grooming—the plush coated variety seems to shed less. PLUSH: The plush variety has a close fitting double coat of medium coarse guard hairs, with a softer undercoat. The head and muzzle, back of the ears and front of the legs and paws are covered with short smooth hairs. The neck has a distinct "mane" that extends to, and covers the chest, with slightly shorter hair covering the remaining torso, not to exceed 5" in length. The "feathering" inside of the ears and on the back of the forelegs should not exceed 3" in length. Show Grooming should include the trimming of all excess fur from between the toes, around the pads, and the removal of all "tufts" from among the "feathering" inside the ears.

MINOR FAULTS
1. Undue length between the last rib and thigh when viewed from the side.
2. Tails that are too short, thin or ratty.
3. Any white markings on any part of the body, excluding the chest and toes (unless all white, then other or faded markings covering the white should be penalized).
4. When in motion any back that does not remain firm, but displays a sway, whip, or roach.
5. An uneven topline when standing, with the withers lower than the croup.

VERY SERIOUS FAULTS
1. Spooking at strange sights or sounds, along with tucking under of tail.
2. Faults of gait, whether from front, rear, or side.
3. Ears that are too large in proportion to the head, show signs of weakness, or point "east-west" away from the center of the head.
4. Any coat that is open, woolly, curly, too close or too long.
5. Splay and/or hare feet, weak and/or cowhocks.
6. A tail that forms a hook or ring when relaxed.

DISQUALIFYING FAULTS

1. Any male (over 36 months) measuring less than 28" or female (over 36 months) measuring less than 26."
2. Dogs over 15 months of age with hanging ears.
3. Any adult dogs with a distinctly overshot or undershot bite.
4. A tail that is raised above the vertical line and/or past the horizontal line of the croup.

SCALE OF POINTS FOR JUDGING

1) General Appearance	strength, size, balance	15
2. Character	alertness and attitude	5
3. Head & Ears	eyes, teeth, & neck	15
4. Forequarters	wither, leg, feet, toes	10
5. Proportion	body, chest, ribs, abdomen	10
6. Topline, Tail, Hindquarters		15
7. Gait, Transmission		25
8. Color, Coat		5
		100

The full Shiloh Shepherd Illustrated Breed Standard, with 71 custom drawings commissioned by the members of the Shiloh Shepherd Dog Club of America, Inc., may be viewed in the Shiloh Shepherd Learning Center at www.shilohshepherds.info/issrIllustratedBreedStandard.htm.

Photo Credits

Photos on the following pages are from the Tina M. Barber collection: xvi, 19, 20, 37, 43 (top), 44, 47, 49, 55, 70, 74, 81, 90 (bottom), 93, 99, 101, 109, 119 (both), 127, 133, 135, 140, 151, 172 (top), 174.

Photos on the following pages are from the Anita DePola collection: xviii, 2, 4 (top), 14, 39, 40, 53, 61, 65, 71, back cover (portrait of Tina).

Photos on the following pages are from the Shiloh Shepherds Kennel Newsletter: 8, 13, 18, 45, 67, 72.

Photos on the following pages are from the Karen Ursel collection: 25, 43 (bottom), 113 (right), 143, 144, 165 (both), 169, 172 (bottom), 173 (right), 175, back cover (William Lee Golden and Charley).

Lisa Barber collection: 113 (left), 122.

Photos on pages 155-162 were submitted by the letters' authors.

Other Photo Credits:

iii, Carrie Hemlock of Hemlock Photography, Ashland, Kentucky.

xvii, Shiloh Kennel brochure.

3, Mr. Pavel Hanuska.

5 (bottom), *The German Shepherd Dog in Word and Picture* by Max Von Stephanitz, p, 629.

10, NASA logo from NASA advertisement in *German Shepherd Dog Review*, March 1978, page 68.

24, Fred Lanting.

30 & 31, Shiloh Shepherd Kennel Stockbook.

84, Chuck Eisenmann.

87, International Shiloh Shepherd Registry, Inc.

89 & 117, Shiloh Shepherd Dog Club of America, Inc. (SSDCA, Inc.) Newsletter.

90 (bottom), SSDCA, Inc. mailing.

96, Christine Rydzeski.

107, Bruce Harkin.

126, Scott Vrooman Sr.

149, Jessica Schepler.

172 (left), from a portrait of Shep painted by Lou Wilson.

Front Cover: designed by Larry Harris. Photos: Tom Gunther, Tina M. Barber and Karen Ursel.